DYNAMICS OF DEVELOPMENT AND PLANNING

DYNAMICS OF DEVELOPMENT AND PLANNING

Mizoram a Comprehensive Regional Analysis

GIRINDRA KUMAR

KALPAZ

Dynamics of Development and Planning : Mizoram a
Comprehensive Regional Analysis

ISBN: 978-81-7835-905-2

Published in 2012 in India by
Kalpaz Publications
C-30, Satyawati Nagar,
Delhi-110052
E-mail: kalpaz@hotmail.com
Phone : 9212729499

Lasser Type Setting by: Rudra Computer Graphics, Delhi
Printed at : Chawla Offset Press, Delhi

Contents

PART - III

List of Figures

PLATE

List of Tables

Preface

The present book owes its origin to the belief that 'diversely different citizenry of a country like India (especially, as the noble laureate Mohammad Yunus puts it in economic terms, the poorest 50% of it) if informed of the causality and interconnectedness of different phenomena in areas of their abode, will be better equipped to decide and extricate itself from the misery of hunger and poverty. Appreciation of environmental constraints and accordant activities may also help them preserve their 'identity' and 'self respect' for it will empower them to remove the 'ignobility of 'being directed' and of 'being dependent' under adopted development strategies. The book also engages with the institutional arrangements under the prevailing systems of governance which is found to be causing 'development of underdevelopment' at greater pace accentuating the interpersonal as well as regional differences. It is high time that the academics, both present and future, attempt to critically analyze the growth and development and their implications in the light of geographical reality that embraces in it the physical and social conditions as well as the cultural attributes of a region.

The views expressed in this book were formed by my training in traditional geography courses and over thirty six years of my association with underdeveloped tribal societies in

Northeast India. Mizoram, one of the most developed states on chosen social parameters, was selected as a case study because economic and social differentiations in the state appear to be getting increasingly more entrenched. Due to lack of understanding of the geo-spatial processes on the part of the people the state appears to be failing in broadening its economic base and compromising with ideologies alien to it.

The book is designed for the students and researchers of social sciences, regional and political economy and modern history who may like to have at least broader view of operations that impinge on regional processes of development and wellbeing of the people. It is also hoped that the students of geography, in tune with the synthetic nature of the subject and as spatial scientists in making, will be benefitted more as the book, to the best of my ability, is prepared in the tradition of geographical writings. It, however, is for the user of the book to assess its utility either as course book or as a guide manual to the processes of planning and development.

Girindra Kumar

Prologue

Geography as a science of spatial organization is essentially concerned with regions regions that go through the process of evolution with varied degree of nature and human interactions. They as a result emerge as unique entities. More often than not, however, writings on regional geographies are found to emphasize the description of 'static features and patterns as determined by the nature'. The interactive relationship of socio-economic and political factors intertwined with natural processes and its dynamism lending personality to a region, is generally overlooked. It is more explicit in terms of development discourse.

The concept of development (though the term in its present sense is a legacy of post 2nd World War era in development thinking), it requires to be noted, has passed through many phases under recasting of economic models' since the dawn of mercantilism in 16-17th century. The classical political economists like Adam Smith propagated capital accumulation through 'selfish economic drive' in an environment of free trade with no artificial impediments. Others from Ricardo to Marx also addressed the question of development through restructuring of the relationship between agriculture and industry to bring about economic growth (till recently equated with development).

Colonial economic philosophy of late 19th and early 20th century (considered to be the immediate predecessor of modern development thinking) was based on optimization of 'cost effectiveness' of resources and 'colonial resource management' which would spill over lateral benefits to the people in the countries of operation.

Neoclassical economists in tune with the demands of macroeconomics assigned greater importance to economic growth based on utilitarian production centered on creation of demand and consumption, competitive market and capital-output ratio. Dissatisfied with the neoclassical model which failed to satisfy demands of the relationship between employment and production system controlled only by market mechanism Keynesyian growth theory, developed during the Great Depression of 1930s, adopted a doctrine of multiplier effects on consumption through propensity, accelerator effect on investment and government intervention in the market according to relevant social policies. It assumed 'improvement in people's working capacities would lead to growth in real wages hence the standard of living' through the process of 'trickle down' to the mass of population. The doctrine of comparative advantage and trade theories enshrined in neoclassical economic thought was, however, found to favour core industrial countries against peripheral agricultural ones wherein global economic regulation was intended to be directed by the rich, the powerful and the European.

Growth of post colonial development thinking originating mainly from Latin America, Asia and Africa emphasized the autocentricity of the main stream economics and its failure to address social and community problems which varied in different ecological settings. It required development thinking to incorporate multilevel, multiscaral regional attributes within a country against macroeconomic measures of nations and beyond. The idea may be regarded as the fore runner of Regional analysis and planning aiming to engineer greater parity amongst the different sections of population in different regions at national and international levels. However, development thinking has always been 'under the shadow of Western Hegemony'. 'The hegemonic effect' R. W. Cox opines in his paper entitled "Gramsci, Hegemony and International Relations: An Essay in Methods (1991, Millennium 12 (2): 162 75) 'occurs both at national and international levels through which developed societies attempt to homogenize different cultural groups' in utter disregard to their environment and social values. United Nations Development Program (UNDP) recognized this malady and thus incorporated in the ambit of development capacitation through enlargement of human choice in respect of access to knowledge, nutrition and health services, security, leisure with political and cultural freedoms through structural adjustments. However, dependence on exogenous assistance is found to be far from attaining the goals. In developing economies, it is found to have deepened the divide between the rich and the poor and seems to have bred corruption and inefficiency. Human dignity must be earned it cannot be bestowed upon. It also reflects the failure of Regional Development thinkers who unwittingly have been emulating models and their variants from conventional economics without any significant success to reduce interpersonal/interregional disparities. It must be realized that in prevailing politico-economic situation under neoliberal economic thinking which is believed by Jan Nederveen Pieterse (Development Theory: Deconstructions/Reconstructions (2001); Vistaar Pub; Delhi) to be a return to neoclassical economics and 'elimination of the foundation of development economics' by limiting 'market distorting intervention of the governments'. Onus, therefore, falls on the people who must come forward to take responsibilities to improve their own lot.

It is in this light that the format of the present book was envisaged. Hence, the title 'Dynamics of Development and Planning: Mizoram, A Comprehensive Regional Analysis'. A modest attempt has been made to correlate the aspects that are basic to the 'landscape evolution' in the state of Mizoram and its development. Mizoram has been selected for this kind of study because the state has been exposed to different development strategies relatively recently. Man- environment relationship has not yet assumed a complexity that developed areas are experiencing. It has hardly been 125 years when the tribal populace of Mizoram started departing from their innate dependence on nature that necessitated restructuring of the relationship. Substantial changes have taken place since. The change over, however, appears not only to have been disturbing the balance of man-nature relationship it is also stretching the capacity of human occupancy of the area in its totality, economic resources, welfare measures for the community and available infrastructure. In short, all aspects that is relevant to attain betterment of the people.

There may, however, be shortcomings in interpretation given though attempt has been made to do so under conceptual frameworks relevant to regional studies. It has been my attempt to maintain objectivity. The views expressed in different chapters may not, however, be entirely in conformity with the views of many. In fact, one purpose of the present endeavour is to agitate the mind of its users. It may help to seek better and more plausible explanations with empirical evidences of the existing and prospective relationship of various phenomena relevant to regional analysis.

The book, I believe, will cater to the needs of the students and broaden their horizon in understanding the geographical, economic and socio-cultural realities of different regions in general and the state and its people in particular. For the convenience of interpretation and understanding the book has been divided in three parts The Land, The People and The Economy. It is believed to provide a comprehensive systematic account of the geography of Mizoram under theoretical constructs that are commonly accepted. I, therefore, believe that the book will help students to understand the evolution of regional landscapes on global level. Moreover, the book also underlines the ecological significance of phenomena that I believe must form the part of any geographical writing. If there is any misrepresentation of the facts, the responsibility is entirely mine.

I'll fail in my duties if I do not acknowledge the supports and helps rendered to me. I am indebted to my wife Smt. Gauri who had constantly been coercing me to contribute something substantial for the people amongst whom I live and work. Without her inspiration, untiring support and encouragement this book would not have seen the light of the day. I am also thankful to my two sons Gaurav and Gahan, who deal with people and happenings nationally and internationally as executives in their respective vocations. They have always been helping me in maintaining objectivity over long telephonic discussions and helped in having insight in the problems of different regions.

I owe my heartfelt gratitude to all my colleagues who helped me in concretizing my ideas. My heartfelt thanks are due to Shri S. K. Ghosh, a very senior faculty member of the Department of Economics for explaining economic concepts and their significance and his son Devajyoti Ghose who has been helping me with the technalities of computer application. I owe a lot of gratitude to Dr. Shiv Kumar who has been guide and supervisor in the preparation of manuscript and its formatting. I am also thankful to Mrs. Shiv Kumar who wore with us over our long sittings with computer. I am also grateful to the subordinate staff of the Department Ms. Kapthangi, Ms. Lalliankimi, Mr. Lalruatkima, and Mr. Vanlalhmuaka, who took extra trouble to help me in the preparation of manuscript and maps and diagrams of publication quality. Without their dedicated support probably I would not have been able to submit the manuscript for publication.

And last but not the least I am thankful to my students and local friends who helped me in peeping through the history, society and ethos of the people of Mizoram.

Girindra Kumar
Aizawl

Introduction

Location

Located in the eastern part Mizoram is one of the members of the group of states that is commonly designated as the Seven Sisters of North East India. The state earlier known as the Lushai Hills formed one of the districts of Assam since British times and continued to be so even after the reorganization of the Indian States in 1956. Following demands for recognition as an independent political entity during mid 1960s, however, the district dominated by the Mizo tribal was given Union Territory status in1972 as Mizoram - the land of the Mizos. It ultimately became the 24th state of the Indian Union on 20th February 1987 following a Peace Accord signed between the hostile MNF leader Mr. Laldenga and the Government of India on 30th June 1986. The state commands a geographical area of about 21087 km lying between 21°15′-24°35′ N latitudes and 92°15′- 93°29′ E longitudes.*

**Dr. Rintluanga Pachuau, Lecturer in Geography, Pachhunga University College, Aizawl;. Asserts that the location of Mizoram is 21°56′ to 24°31′ N Latiitudes and 92°16′ to 93°26‘ E longitudes; Kawiah nge Mizoram in Dah!, Mizoram Science Journal (1993) (In Mizo Language): August, pp. 11-15: Also see Geography of Mizoram (1994) : Dr. Rintluanga Pachuau, R.T. Enterprise, Aizawl.*

The Tropic of cancer (23°30′ N latitude) bisects Mizoram in almost two equal halves in its 285 km north-south stretch. It extends about 115 km from east to west at its maximum. It is bounded by the Cachar district of Assam and the state of Manipur in the northern part, Myanmar in the east as well as in the south and Bangladesh along with the state of Tripura in

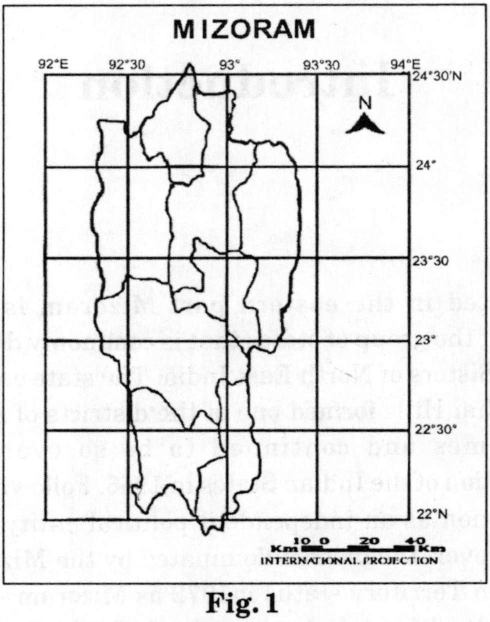

Fig. 1

the west. Apart from having an independent ethnic identity, its location along the sensitive international boundary makes the state strategically important and politically significant. It shares a common boundary of about 404 km with Myanmar and 318 km with Bangladesh.

Such a location assumes greater importance in the light of the people of the same stock living across the border- the Mizos in Myanmar and the Chakmas in Bangladesh. It adds to the political as well as economic dimensions of Mizoram.

NOMENCLATURE

Mizoram, the nomenclature adopted and accepted by the people as well as the constitution of India is derived from the combination of two words - Mizo and Ram. The term Mizo stands for the inhabitants of the hills and ram for country or land. It would literally mean "the land of the highlanders". Derivation of the name is obscured in historical antiquity. The word Mizo, however, is generally beleived to have its close association with the term either Miayao or Miatzu (Miao+yao or tzu) used by the Chinese people to refer to the tribes that inhabited the hills of Yunnan, Szechwan, northern Laos, northern parts of Vietnam and Thailand (Sangkima;1998:20). The expression Zo or Jo was probably first used by the Chinese diplomats of the Tang Dynasty only in 862 A.D. to refer to the princes and chiefs of a particular kingdom which ruled in Chindwin valley and adjoining Chin hills (Vumson; 1986:1). It had only been after the annexation of Bengal by the British that Tom Lewin, an officer in the army ranks, advocated the use of a generic term Dzo (a Burmese synonym for chin) for the tribes who occupied these parts in successive waves of migration in almost 700 years and had distinct identities. Till then, such tribes misleadingly were identified with the latest but the strongest and most dominant of the groups – the Lusheis, who most likely entered the Indian parts only in the 2nd half of the 17th century. It must have been their dominance that led the British administrators to name these parts of eastern hill ranges as Lushai Hills. The area continued to be known as such despite Lewin's attempt to provide more rational identity to the people who believed and claimed to have different ethnography made distinctive during different phases of their migration. Even after the Independence of India the area continued to be known as Lushai Hills. It was not until 1954 (1st September, 1954) that the area was renamed as Mizo District by an Act of the Indian Parliament. It was considered, following the local tradition, to be more inclusive and expressive of the linkages amongst the tribes and sub-tribes of common descent. It was only in 1972 that the Mizo district till then under the province of Assam was granted Union Territory status and attained a distinctive name – Mizoram, the Land of the Highlanders.

Historical Evolution

Incursion of some clans of Mizo tribes in Indian parts is suggested to have started as early as 11th century (Vumson, 1986: 29; Lalrinawma, 1995: 6-7). These clans are believed to have immigrated in successive waves over a period of 600-700 years to occupy their present habitat (Burman, 1970: 100-11; Dalton, 1975: 110-11; Sopitt, 1976: vii-viii; Sangkima,1998: 52-53). In the process of migration the Mizo clans had to adopt a system of administration that was perceived to facilitate and regulate movements, ensure safety to its members, manage the occupied areas and overcome hurdles posed by intense competition and opposition. Administration in traditional Mizo society revolved round the chief of the clan. Closely knit clan based social structure is believed to have led to a system of governance that would be "accepted to both the ruler and the ruled" Each village chief was supposed to be "courageous and wise so as to guide, protect and govern those within his territorial jurisdiction". A chief had to look after the welfare of his people in order to retain them because number of his subject would determine his strength and honor amongst the community of villages in the neighbourhood. If the villagers felt they were being oppressed or were insecure they "had the freedom to move to the jurisdiction of other chiefs". Power to invoke such a freedom gave the villagers unique and sufficient control over the chiefs and was deterrent enough on the arbitrary use of power by them – the supreme governing authority. Thus, even without "any written fundamental laws and principles to prescribe the nature, functions and limits of governance" people were "aware of their rights, duties and privileges as members of the society" (Kyndiah, 1999: 25) and had the power to exercise them. Capt. T.H. Lewin in his encounter with the Mizos in early days of British regime considered the type of governance as "democracy tempered by disposition" (quoted by Kyndiah, 1999: 25) in which 'condition for equality and respect for individual' existed. The chief was, therefore, compelled to seek assistance from experienced and wise members of the clan – the members who were vocationally significant in maintenance of security and in growing agrarian economy.

The Mizo way of administration and organization, however, started undergoing changes when the North and South Lushai hills were amalgamated and formally annexed to British India on 6th September, 1895. The area was put under the administration of the province of Assam on 1st April, 1898 under one Superintendent. Maj. John Shakespeare became the first administrator of the Lushai Hills. Functions of the superintendent were envisaged to be limited to safeguard the interests of the British Empire and security of its personnels. But, in course of time, the British rulers in connivance with the chiefs of the villages extended its authority in matters of taxation and adjudication of justice. A phase, thus, started of limitation on individual freedom and oppressive administration. In the mean time exposure of the local tribal groups to the areas beyond, firstly through the teachings of the Christian missionaries and secondly due to their participation in the 1st and 2nd World Wars in different capacities, led them to revolt against the repressive conditions. The Government of India Act, 1935 worsened the situation that declared the Lushai Hills District to be an 'excluded area'. The provincial government of Assam was not supposed to interfere in the affairs of the area and budgetary allocation for; it was not to be voted in the state assembly because no representative from the area was supposed to be its member. This apparently hampered the expansion of economic activities hence development of the Lushai Hills and welfare of its residents. It culminated in Mizo Civil Disobedience Movement in 1948, immediately after India attained its independence. The situation though improved a little after the First Five Year Plan was adopted in 1952. The Lushai Hills district, then a constituent of the state of Assam benefited marginally. The Movement, however, was aimed basically at abolition of chieftainship. It demanded institution of elected village councils. The objective of the Movement was realized in

1954 through invocation of the Assam Lushai Hills District (Acquisition of Chiefs Rights) Act, 1954.

Lack of infrastructure in these hills, however, did not allow much expansion of economic activities. It remained virtually an 'excluded area'. The problem was further aggravated by the terrible famine 'Mautam' that hit the area in late fifties. People were exposed to unprecedented hardships. In order to combat the disastrous effects of the famine 'Mizo National Famine Front (MNFF) was formed in 1960. The organization, however, changed its name to Mizo National Front (MNF) on 22nd October 1961 and assumed the role of a political party (Kyndiah, 1999:27). Dissatisfied with the functioning of the administrative machineries of the state and perceived apathy of the Union Government the MNF took up arms on 28th February 1966. This heralded the beginning of almost 20 years of unabated bloody conflict. It was also made out to be a cessation movement asking for independent identity. Thus, hostilities between the MNF and Indian security forces continued almost unabated till 1986.

In the mean time, realizing the problem and its multi ethnic composition, the Parliament of India gave assent to reorganization of the northeastern region. As a result, Lushai Hills District of Assam renamed as Mizoram was given Union Territory Status on 21st January 1972. The state was divided into three district administrations of Aizawl, Lunglei, and Saiha for smooth administrative functioning. The new status of Mizoram though did not pacify the insurgent group, it certainly paved the path for further negotiations and the Peace Accord of 1986 signed between the MNF leader Mr. Laldenga and the Government of India. As a condition of the accord, Mizoram acquired status of full statehood on 20th February 1987.

With the realization of responsibilities towards its people, growing development activities and compulsions of administration, the state affected reorganization of its administration again in 1998. The state presently has been organized to have eight districts with smaller areas to facilitate

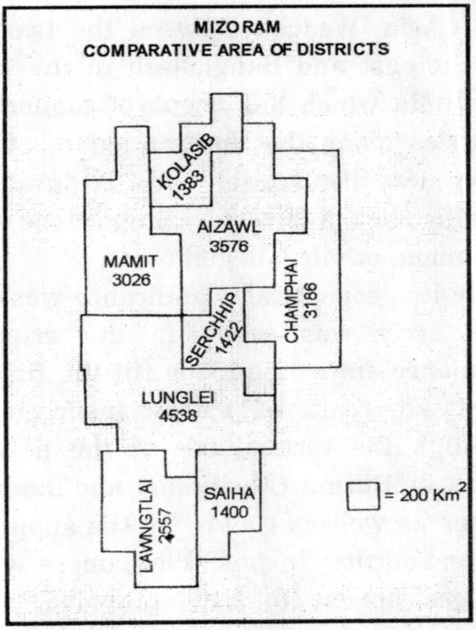

Fig. 2

smooth administrative functions in difficult hill terrain. Fig. 2 provides an idea about the territorial extent of each district.

The state also has three Autonomous District Councils to serve the interests of exclusive tribal groups. Administrative structure developed in the state also provides administration to rural areas through 22 Rural Development Blocks (4 more R. D. Blocks have been notified between 2004 and 2006). Each R. D. Block, on an average, administers 998 sq. km. Reorganization of administrative units with an objective to equitably diffuse economic and development activities is expected to bring about prosperity to the people of Mizoram and maintenance of peace that the state symbolizes with particular reference to prevailing socio-political turmoil that has besieged other states of North east India.

Geo-political Significance

Mizoram commands a unique location especially with reference to the evolving econo - political situation in south and south-east Asia. Wedged between the two countries of Myanmar in the east and Bangladesh in the west it is the only state in India which has people of common descent in the two countries along the international boundary. Even along the inter state boundaries with Tripura, Assam, and Manipur significantly a sizeable proportion of people are bound by common ethnic allegiance.

Militarily its geopolitical significance was realized very little till the state was caught in the grips of violent political turbulence since late 1960s till the first half of the 1980s. Almost 20 years of bloody insurgency could be sustained through the tactical use of the passages to and from the areas in Burma (Myanmar) and Bangladesh that afforded shelter as well as routes for the supply of arms to the underground outfits. In post Vietnamese war the same kind of passages appear to have provided safe haven to illicit trading that makes Mizoram a bastion in the golden triangle – infamous for trafficking in drugs and arms. Despite a very strong civil society the state hardly seem to be able to curb and control the routes of the great menace. It may be attributed to the porosity of the boundaries.

References

Burman, B.K.R (1990) : *Demographic and Social-Economic Profiles of the Hill Areas of North East India*; New Delhi.

Dalton, E.T. (1971) : *Descriptive Ethnology of Bengal; Kolkata.*

Kyndiah, P.R. (1999) : *Pillars of Mizo Society and Thoughts to Share*; Government of Mizoram; Aizawl.

Lalrinawma (1995) : *Mizoram: History and Cultural Identites;* Spectrum, Guwahati.

Pachuau R. (1993) : 'Khawiah nge Mizoram in Dah?' *Mizoram Science Jouranal (in Mizo);* Also in Geographyof Mizoram (1994); R.T. Enterprise; Aizawl.

Sangkima (1998) : *Essays on the History of the Mizos*; Spectrum; Guwahati.

Sopitt (1976) : *A Short Account of Kuki-Lushai Tribes*; Aizawl.

Vumson (1986) : *Zo History;* Aizawl.

PART - I

THE LAND

1

The Land

Physiography:

Topography of the land exerts direct influence on the distribution of various phenomena through altitude, ruggedness and slope. It constitutes a truly foundational resource (Glendinning and Logan, 1959). It influences farming through modification of climate. It also affects the ease of cultivation and degree of farming (Singh, 1976). Therefore, 'plans for regional development should include geographical analysis of the elements of total landscape complex that are relevant to the direction which development is intended to follow' (Thomas, 1969). It is nowhere as essential as in areas where people strive to augment productivity and the process of development. As the form of terrain influences economic use of the land it impinges on the form of socio-cultural organization of the group that inhabits it hence the process of development. It is more evident in Mizoram where all facets of life appear to have been influenced by the terrain attributes. Exploitation of land resources and pattern of their use are directly influenced by different landform characteristics. So, are influenced peopling and pattern of settlements. Fig. 3 indicates the distribution of area at different elevations in Mizoram.

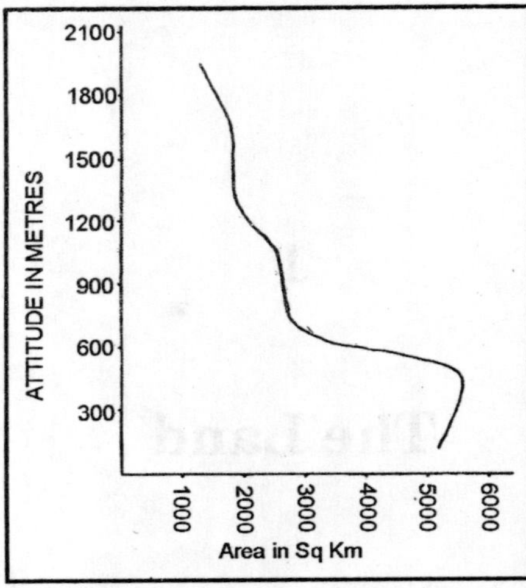

Fig. 3 (a)

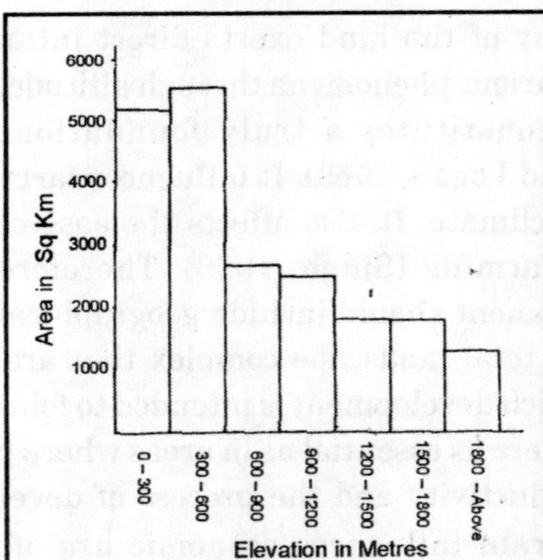

Fig. 3 (b)

Predominantly a hilly terrain, the state of Mizoram is characterized by a north- south alignment of hill ranges (Fig. 4&5). They are separated from each other by narrow river valleys. These valleys, however, open out gradually towards the Barak valley in the north and Koladan valley of Myanmar in the south Evolved as a result of post Miocene and Oilgocene

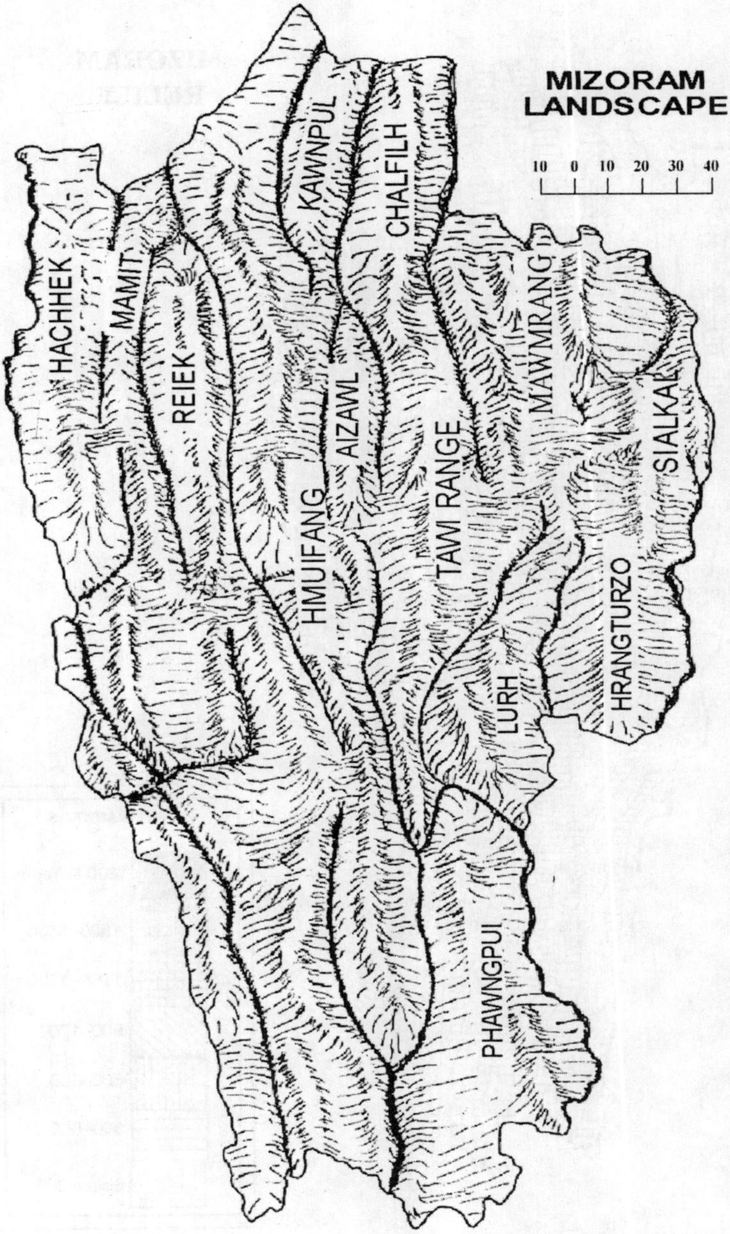
MIZORAM
LANDSCAPE
10 0 10 20 30 40
HACHHEK
MAMIT
REIEK
KAWNPUL
CHALFILH
AIZAWL
HMUIFANG
TAWI RANGE
MAWMRANG
SIALKAL
HRANGTURZO
LURH
PHAWNGPUI

Fig. 4

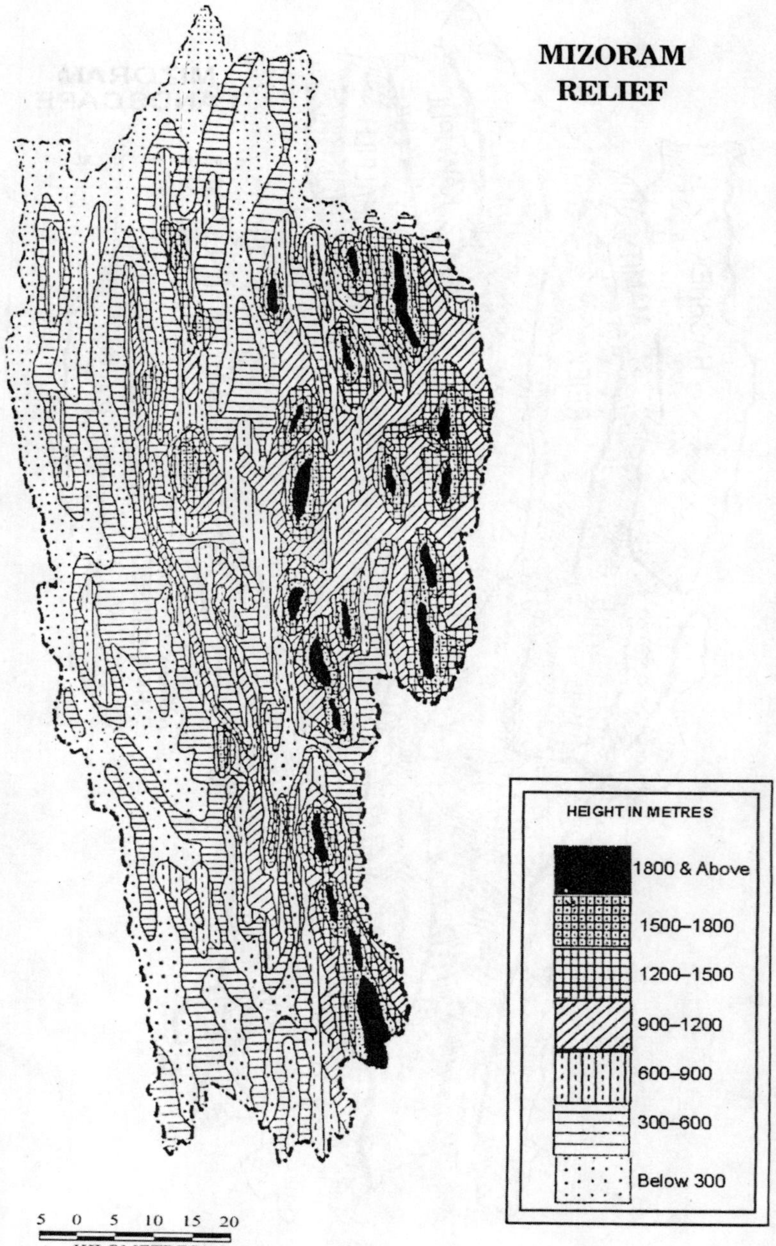
MIZORAM
RELIEF
HEIGHT IN METRES
1800 & Above
1500–1800
1200–1500
900–1200
600–900
300–600
Below 300
5 0 5 10 15 20
KILOMETRES

Fig. 5

thrust of the Himalayan orogeny, the Mizo hills exhibit alternate arrangement of folding along a north-south axis. These ranges generally taper in the north and south. They are relatively broad and higher in their central part that separates north and south flowing rivers.

Gradual evolution of land and varied formations in a short geological history of the region has left distinct imprints on the structure and relief of the area. On the basis of structural and relief characteristics, therefore, the state may broadly be divided into three physiographic units though they may not be very distinct in their spatial distribution- (i)Eastern High Hills ; (ii) The Western Low Hills; and (iii) Intermontane flat lands.

1. Eastern High Hills: Hills in Mizoram form an integral part of a mobile belt. The region is supposed to be forming the tectonic section associated with eastward subduction of the Indian plate at its Arakan Yoma margin. The Eocene orogeny and subsequent thrust are considered to be responsible for folding of Indo-Burma (Myanmar) ranges of mountains (Nandi, 1982). The folds, thus, form a distinct part of a mobile belt having a marked sub-meridional trend along a north –south axis. The ranges represent anticline that alternate with saucer shaped synclines (Fig. 4). They are slightly arcuate along the axis of folds. The folds are transacted by numerous longitudinal faults and thrusts. The westward convexity of the folded ranges may be attributed to these longitudinal faults and thrusts that transverse the north-south trending folds. The hills in general are formed of compact and resistant older rocks along the anticline crests. The intervening synclinal valleys, on the other hand, exhibit younger and softer formations (Ganguly, 1983). Hill ranges in Mizoram are distinct and form the watersheds between various river basins and sub- basins. They are characterized by a declining altitudinal trend from east to west. Generally, however, six ranges may be identified in the state as follows:

1. The Sialkal- Hrangturzo Range: 2. The Chalfilh-Tawi-Lurh-Phawngpui Range; 3. The kawnpui- Aizawl- Hmuifang Range: 4. the Reiek Range; and 5. the Hachhek – Mamit Range.

(i) The Sialkal- Hrangturzo Range: The two hill ranges together form the eastern most and highest hill ranges in the state along the border with Manipur and Myanmar. In fact, the Sialkal range along the Manipur boarder forms a watershed between south flowing R. Tiau along the Myanmarese boarder in the east and R. Tuipui in the west. These ranges generally rise above 1500 meters from the sea level. The elevation in this range, however, varies from about 400 meters in narrow river valleys to more than 2100 meters. Some of the highest peaks of the state like Longteng (2149 m), Nunuarzo (2140 m) and Sur (2018 m) are found in this range.

The Sialkal range is separated from a much smaller range of Mawmrang by the valley of Tuivai. In its short run from the northern boundary of the state with Manipur the range acts as a water divide between R. Tuivai in the east and R. Tuivawl in the west. The average height of this range varies from 1200 to 1800 meters from the mean sea level.

(ii) The Chalfilh – Tawi – Lurh – Phawngpui Range: The Chalfiah and Tawi ranges of central Mizoram may be considered to have its continuation through Lurh Range in South-eatern parts along the Myanmar boarder where it is named as Phawngpui Range. The disruption in the continuation of the northern ranges towards the south appears to have been affected by the confluence of R. Tuichang and R. Mat, the two tributaries to the south flowing R. Chhimtuipui as well as R . Tuipui, another tributary. The Lurh Range occupies the space between R. Tuipui and R. Tuichang. River Tuichang distinguishes the higher Lurh Range from lower Tawi Range. As a matter of fact, R. Chimtuipui which flows in a northerly direction along the Myanmar- Indian border as R. Koladine enters Mizoram flowing in a westerly direction and marks the division between Lurh – Tawi, the northern ranges on one hand and the Phawngpui Range of the south on the other.

In the northern part R. Tuivawl separates the Chalfilh Range from the eastern Mawmrang Range. The Tawi Range makes the watershed between R. Tuichang in the east and R.

Mat in the west. The Chalfilh and the Tawi ranges have an elevation of over 1900 and 1800 meters respectively. The highest peak in the state the Phawngpui (Blue Mountains), however, is located in the Phawngpui Range, in the Eastern part of Saiha district, where it attains a height of about 2157 meters.

These ranges exhibit distinctive relief characteristics. Though lower in elevation than the eastern Sialkal Range variability of relief and steepness of slopes are marked in these ranges. More than half of the area occupied by these ranges has a slope of more than 50 per cent, a feature that is detrimental to rational land utilization by the people of the area.

(iii) The Kawnpui- Aizawl - Hmuifang range: These ranges form the Central axis of the state. It is separated from the eastern Chalfilh –Tawi Ranges by the Valleys of north flowing R. Tuirial and South flowing R. Mat. The ridge tops are generally wider and slopes relatively gradual when compared to eastern ranges. Occasionally, however, the ridge tops attain heights over 1800 meters from the sea level.

These ranges have the distinction to house many large settlements as the national highway NO. 54 from Silchar to Saiha through Aizawl and Lunglei occupies most of its run along these ranges.

(iv) The Reiek range: The Reiek Range between north flowing R. Tlawng and R. Tut is bounded in the north by their confluence. It runs southward almost as a continuous range till the southern boundary of Mizoram is crossed. In its southern stretch the range is bounded by south flowing tributaries of R. Chhimtuipui and north flowing R.Tuichang. Belted as a narrow range in the north the range becomes much wider and slopes towards the two major river valleys of Chhimtuipui and Tuichang much more gradually. The highest ridges in this range vary from a height of 900 m. to 1200 m. However, the western flanks of these ranges exhibit relatively greater steepness where it terminates in R. Tut valley with less than 300 m. of height from the sea level. On the eastern margin except for northern part bounded by R. Tlawng, the range joins the Aizawl range through a synclinal valley which generally has a height just over 500 meters.

Despite low absolute relief both western and specially the eastern slopes present a very rugged and hostile condition. It hampers the accessibility to settlements in this part. Naturally exploitation and productive use of local resources are handicapped.

(v) The Hachhek- Mamit Range: The Hachhek – Mamit Range along the western boundary of the state represents protuberances in an otherwise low lying topography of the western lowlands. The height rarely exceeds 900 m. with the exception of the central portion where some of the peaks attain heights mostly in northern parts even above 1300 m. In the southern parts generally the maximum height is limited by 600 m. contours. The range is bounded by north flowing R. Teirei and border river Langkhai in the north and R. Tuichawng in the south. The hill ranges generally have relatively broad tops and wider flanks that imperceptibly mingle with the lowlands occupied by valleys of various rivers.

The Hachhek range runs parallel to the Mamit range separated from it by the valley of R. Terei and Marlui. The two ranges continue in southern Mizoram. Their continuity is broken by the headwaters of R. Teirei and westerly course of R. Deh and R. Tuichawng that debouch the Chittagong Hill Tracts in Bangladesh. The range continues further south and forms a watershed between R. Tuichawng in the east and R. Kawrpui that acts as a boundary between Mizoram and Bangladesh.

2. The Western Lowlands: There exists a low lying area along the western boundary and along the northern slopes of hill ranges in Mizoram that terminates in the Cachar Plains. The valleys of R. Tut along with that of R. Teirei, R. Serlui in the northern and in the west and southern R. Deh, R. Marlui and R. Tuichwang coalesce to form the parts of this lowland.

The surface manifestation of this low lying area, however, is disturbed by the presence of low altitude and broken ridges that also include the Mamit-Hachchat hill ranges. Lying between the Chittagong Hill Tracts of Bangladesh and the Mizo hills, this low lying area has characteristics of an intermontane plain with greater integration of river systems. The surface features exhibit characteristics of erosion and retreat of mountainous slopes. It is evident from the presence of gravel and thickly bedded sand stones that dominate the sediments in this part of the state.

In northern part, in the basin of R. Teirei a small patch of alluvial plain distinguishes itself from the adjoining plains. In all probability it is a depositional plain - an extension of the Cachar plains. Other adjoining lowlands within the northern boundary of Mizoram exhibit the features of erosion as different formations of Surma series of rocks are exposed on the surface. In fact, the alluvial plain of the Teirei Basin is a very recent formation that unconformably overlies the Surma formation of late Oligocene to mid- Miocene period.

Average elevation in this part of the state is about 700 meters from the sea level but the local relief may vary between 40 to 300 meters. The western slopes of the ridges generally are steeper and are marked with greater relief variations.

3. Intermontane Plains: Intermontane plains in Mizoram do not form any continuous patch. They are widely scattered. Therefore, it is difficult to classify them as distinct physical unit. Yet they have structural traits that distinguish them from the hills and the western lowlands of the state. Most of these plains are minuscule in dimension. But they still have significant position in the existing as well as potential development of the state's economy. Sheltered by the hill ranges all around these plains generally exhibit characteristics of lacustrine origin identified with the post Pliestocene period. The soil profiles of these plains possess entirely different attributes from the soils of leached slopes of the hills or transported soils of the river valleys. Sediments in these plains exhibit features of deposition in still waters. It is possible that they owe their formation to orogenic disturbances in the area.

Subsequent silting has made them fertile and suitable for permanent cultivation.

Though such plains are found in different parts of the state, they occur with greater frequency and larger dimensions in the eastern part. Few of such flat lands are easily recognizable. The Champhai valley in the eastern part of Champhai District, the Thenzawl plain south of Aizawl, Vanlaiphai spread over in Serchip and Lunglei Districts and the Chamdur plains in the eastern part of Saiha District represent the few flat lands which play a vital role in the state's economy or have significant potentials. Of these, the Champhai plain is the biggest. It is spread in almost 50 km^2. The second largest plain is that of North Vanlaiphai in Serchip District.

Besides the above mentioned intermontane plains numerous small patches may also be identified in northern, western and central parts of the state. Thus, Tuisen Hnar in the vicinity of Khawzawl, Zawlpui in the Mat river basin, Phaisen chhimluang to the west of Bilkhawthlir, Hortoki and Bairabi in the northern part of the Tlawng river basin are some of the flat patches which may increasingly assume greater significance in the state's agricultural economy. Almost all of these small patches of flat lands presently are given to wet rice cultivation with the only exception of the Chamdur Plains which is still thickly forested and has a very small population to support. In this regard it must be noted that these small plains possibly with the exception of the Champhai and North Vanlaiphai have not been given a proper developmental thrust. Hence they have failed to assume much significance in the economy of the state despite their potential for agricultural use. Nevertheless they are locally important and offer happy respite from traditional slash and burn cultivation.

Geology

The landform in Mizoram is believed to have started evolving during the Tertiary era. Geologists believe that the area belongs to a geosyncline that existed during the Eocene period between the Chittagong Hill Tracts of Bangladesh in the west and the Arakan Yoma of Myanmar in the east. The geosyncline has been named as the Assam Gulf. It persisted till the middle of the Miocene period. This Gulf, most likely, was independent of the northern Tethys and formed part of southern sea (Wadia, 1975:290).

The Tertiary mountain Building revolution that led to the rise of the great Himalaya system of mountains in place of a pre Eocene Tethys sea also led to the formation of a Himalayan fore deep parallel to its southern slopes from Assam to Sind. Later the depression was probably occupied by a great north-west flowing river (Krishnan and Aiyangar, 1940) named the Siwalik (Pilgrim, 1919) or the Indobrahm (Pascoe, 1919) having its headwaters in Assam. The river flowed to the contemporary Sind Gulf in the western part of north India. The Indobrahm basin was separated from the Southern sea by a watershed dividing the northerly drainage from the southward flowing river (Wadia, 1975:51-52). The watershed in Eastern – India was represented by the Assam Range.

Post Siwalik movement in North-West Punjab is accredited to have brought changes in the courses of rivers and dismemberment of the great Indobrahm system. Consequently three subsidiary systems of drainage developed as (a) South flowing present Indus (b) South-westerly courses of the five tributaries of the Indus in Punjab: and (c) The Gangatic system with a southeasterly course (Wadia, 1975:51-52). It is the Ganga-Brahmaputra system of rivers with expansive estuarine and deltaic deposits that are believed to have accelerated the recession and extinction of the Assam Gulf. Due to later weakening thrust associated with the Himalayan Orogeny the sediments deposited in the Gulf are believed to have been folded in a repetitive succession of north-south trending anticlines and synclines that form the Mizo (Lushai) hills.

The lithology of the hills suggests their origin. The Mizo hills are a great thickness of detrital sediments with alternate occurrence of argillaceous and arenaceous deposits. The upper sandstone with occasional clay bands and overlain by recent alluvium represents the fluvial deposits. It attains a thickness of about 950 meters in Mizoram. These deposits range in age from early Pliocene to late Miocene. They represent Tipam series of Assam. They are separated from upper alluvium of recent geological times by an unconformity for, no trace of intervening Pliestocene deposits is found in this area. Generally, however, the lithology is dominated by alternate arenaceous and argillaceous deposits of sandstones, shales and siltstones deposited in a retreating Assam Gulf during Oligocene-Miocene periods. The sediments conform to the marine deposits common to Surma group of rocks. The upper series of Surma rocks may, however, have lacustrine or estuarine origin as is obvious from the fossil collections from the Tipam and the Surmas of Mizoram (Tiwari et al, 1996). Thickness of the Surmas in this part reaches up to 5,000 meters.

The oldest rocks in the state having a thickness of about 3,000 meters are believed to have a marine origin of Oligocene period. They are generally identified as Barail series of rocks though there are many who refute it.

In the light of the above analysis a generalized stratigraphic succession and mode of occurrence may be discerned in Mizoram. Four litho-stratigraphic units have been identified in the state (fig. 6). They in order of their succession may be grouped as follows:-

(i) The Barail series (ii) The Surma series
(iii) The Tipam series (iv) The Alluviums.

(i) The Barails*: the Barail series of rocks represents the oldest formation in Mizoram. They are mostly found along R. Tuichang and R. Tuivai in the eastern part of the state. They may be considered to be the western extension of the Barail segment of the Pegu System of Myanmar uplifted in the post Eocene thrust of the Himalayan Orogeny.

**The occurrence of Barails in Mizoram has been contested. GSI and associated workers like Nandi et al (1983) report the occurrence of Barails in Champhai area whereas ONGC workers, Gunju (1975); Jokhan Ram and Venkataraman (1984) consider it as the part of Surma group.*

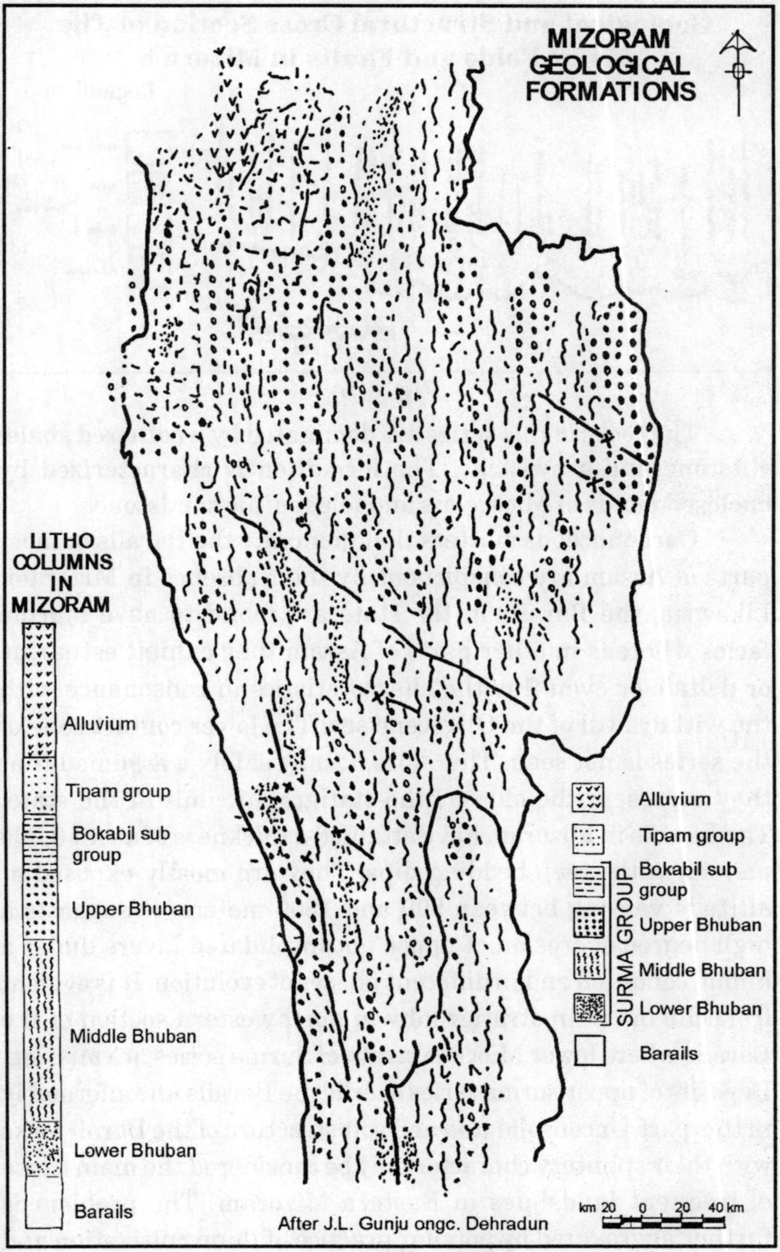
MIZORAM
GEOLOGICAL
FORMATIONS
LITHO
COLUMNS
IN
MIZORAM
Alluvium
Tipam group
Bokabil sub group
Upper Bhuban
Middle Bhuban
Lower Bhuban
Barails
Alluvium
Tipam group
Bokabil sub group
Upper Bhuban
Middle Bhuban
Lower Bhuban
SURMA GROUP
Barails
km 20 0 20 40 km
After J.L. Gunju ongc. Dehradun

Fig. 6(a)

Geological and Structural Cross Section of The Major Folds and Faults in Mizoram

Legend

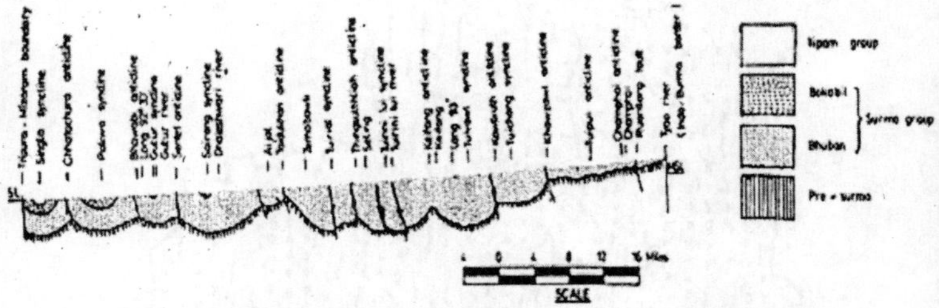

Fig. 6(b)

The rocks of this series are dominated by weathered shale, siltstone and greywacks. The formation is characterized by enclosed bands of Micaceous and feldspathic sandstones.

Carbonaceous matters that dominate the Barails in most parts of Assam are conspicuous by their absence in Mizoram. Likewise, the Barails in the state are found to have marine facies whereas in other parts of Assam they exhibit estuarine or deltaic or even fluvitile characteristics in consonance with the withdrawal of the Oligocene sea. The lower contact zone of the series is not seen. Therefore, it may safely e assumed that they represent the oldest litho-statigraphic unit in the state. The Barails in Mizoram have attained a thickness of about 3,000 meters, with steep bedding dips. They are mostly exposed at altitude varying between 900 and 1800 meters. It suggests a high degree of erosion of upper unconsolidated layers under a humid condition and in different phases of evolution. It is evident from the break in stratigraphy in northwestern section of the Barails where lower Miocene strata of Surma series are missing. Deposits of upper surma series overlie the Barails unconformably in this part.Unconsolidated and soft structure of the Barail rocks with their splintery character may be considered the main cause of frequent landslides in Eastern Mizoram. The problem is further aggravated by popular practice of jhum cultivation and large scale deforestation which lead to further fragmentation and down slope movement of talus both in humid and dry conditions.

(ii) The Surma series: West of the Barails the surface exposure is dominated by the Surma series of rocks in the state. Sandstones admixed with ferruginous materials; mudstone and shale abound in the structure. The nature of rocks, however, varies with altitude. Generally, loose arenaceous sediments are found at higher altitudes and on ridges whereas the synclinal valleys and slopes at lower altitude are predominantly argillaceous.

The Surmas in Mizoram are separated from the earlier deposits of Barails by unconformity (unconformable contact zone, however, appears to have been obliterated due to faulting that accompanied the mid- Miocene orogeny). Three distinct formations of Surma series of rocks corresponding to Bhuban sub-group have been identified in the state. They have alternate arrangements of arenaceous and argillaceous sediments. The lowest of the Surmas-lower Bhuban formation, corresponds with the upper Oligocene. The formation is dominated by arenaceous sandstone and silt shale. They attain a thickness of 900 meters and are most exposed on central and western ridges of Mizoram hills. It appears that the lower deposits have been eroded away owing to steepness of the dipping beds.

The middle Bhuban formation is separated from lower formations through a conformable and transitional belt. The nature of sediments reaching a thickness of about 3,000 meters is, however, argillaceous. Shale, silt shale alterations and sandstones are found almost every where in intermontane valleys and lower slopes of the hills where middle Bhuban formations dominate. Similarly, the upper Bhuban formations reaching a thickness of about 1100 meters are separated from the middle formations through a transitional contact. Only the sediments assume arenaceous traits and occupy higher altitudes.

The latest of the Surma-the Boka Bil formations are exposed only in northern and western parts of the state adjoining Tripura and Chittagong hills respectively. Thickness of the layer has been estimated to be about 950 meters with sandstones, siltstone and shale in order of their succession.

The Surmas in Mizoram correspond mostly to Oligocene-Miocene Sea (Tiwari et al: 1997:127) with possible exception of Boka Bil formation which conformably is mingled with the Tipam series and may have estuarine origin.

(iii) The Tipam Series: Tipam group of sediments is generally limited to northwestern part of the state having an exposed thickness of about 950 meters. In Mizoram the series corresponds to late Miocene to early Pliocene periods. They are characterized by thick, coarse ferruginous sandstone and sandy shale deposits. The series is entirely non-marine and generally have subdued topography and wider stream channels.

(iv) The Alluvial Group: Thin veneer of alluvium deposits in the state conform to the most recent geological times. They overlie the Tipam series of rocks unconformably in the northwestern parts and there is no evidence of Pleistocene period that elapsed in between. The alluvium is also found in narrow river valleys at the confluence of major streams. The deposits are characterized by the presence of silt, clay and gravel.

The Tertiary system of rocks altogether attain a thickness of about 10000 meters though their sequence might have been disturbed due to creation of numerous faults and thrust planes that accompanied the evolution of the Lushai hills in different phases of orogeny. The intensity of the mountain building forces has left indelible mark on the structural attributes of the state. Numerous faults and fault lines criss-cross the region. Many of the faults have been created transverse to the existing hill ranges whereas there are quite a few of them that run parallel to the hill ranges in a north-southerly direction. The faults have complicated the lithology and associated topography in the state on the one hand; they might have adversely affected the occurrence of minerals of any economic significance on the other. However, intensive geological studies are still awaited to comprehend the full significance of the geological sequences and events in the state.

Hydrography

Natural channels for surface flowage-the streams have been a natural source of water for human consumption, agricultural use and transportation. Uses, control and conservation of running water, however, largely depend on the physical-climatic conditions of the regions they traverse. Rock structure, soil types and vegetal cover are important determinants of linear properties of the stream channel system. They swell in response to seasonal downpours. They shrink during the dry spells. They influence the ground water reservoir of the basin they occupy. Excessive rain leading to pronounced gully erosion renders the land useless. Increasing human activities in order to maximize returns from the use of natural resource also impinge not only on the quality but also on the quantity of this most elemental source of water. Irrational use of water upstream may wreak havoc downstream. Sewage outlets of settlements and release of industrial effluent in the neighboring streams have been reported to cause health hazards beyond control. They irreparably damage the aquatic life. Misuses of surface water have been found to contaminate the ground water and render it unusable. In short, the health of the ecosystem besides supply of moisture largely depends on the quality of water and the nature of terrain they develop on.

Streams are also the most potent factor that brings about changes in the landscape especially in wet climates. In tune with the nature of terrain volume and velocity equip the streams with capacity of erosion. Accordingly, they subdue the landforms. As main transporting agents of detrital matters rivers tend to grade their valleys and affect change in longitudinal as well as cross profiles of their course. Gradation is also reflected in increasingly greater integration of channels. They reveal the nature of terrain they criss-cross. An analysis of hydrological conditions prevailing in river basins and its impact on long and cross profiles of stream channels, therefore, gives an insight in the physical processes that operate in tandem. It also helps to understand the evolution of existing structural and geomorphic features of the region. As agents of gradation rivers have immense bearing on land use pattern made increasingly complicated by the rising and varied demands on land. It impinges on the areal attributes, hence the direction of development that is envisaged for the well-being of the people. In a state like Mizoram where all development programme depend on unsustainable Central Government assistance-either financed entirely or in the form of subsidies and aids, plans for development in tune with the physical attributes may have much significance for obvious reasons. River basins, in this regard, may provide the basis for micro level planning for; they are the areal expressions of unified processes that distinguish one watershed from the other. It must also impinge on the human response and adjustments unique to the basins, not necessarily in broad forms but certainly in minute details. Hence, inter basin cultural variance. Such studies, therefore, may have greater importance in the field of sustainable land utilization especially for agriculture, horticulture, and forest development, selection of sites for dams and hydal power installations as well as human habitation. Realization of political autonomy makes it imperative for the planners and executioners of the development programme to take the state forward from a dependent to self-reliant economy. Division of the planning regions of a predominantly agricultural state on the basis of watersheds in this regard may provide a foundation for proper resource utilization and sustainable development. It may also assuage the bitter feelings of communities in remote parts who at present feel to have been marginalized. It may, therefore, be suggested that even administrative units on the basis of watershed compatible with the planning regions are obtained without political expediency. It is expected to ensure more cohesive plan for action, avoid duplicity and delay in execution. This may also lead to greater participation of people enabling them to set their development objectives and evolve processes in tune with the democratic values of the Mizo society.

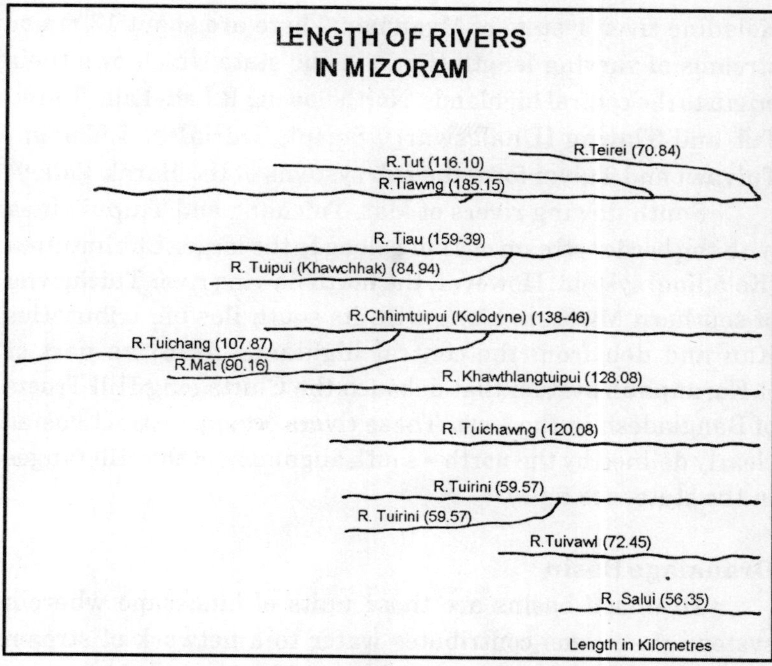

Fig. 7

Rivers of Mizoram are small and generally occupy narrow north-south trending basins. The longest river in the state is R. Tlawng traversing a distance of 185 km. Fig. 6 shows the relative length of important rivers in Mizoram. They may be classified in two broad groups as – (i) north flowing, and (ii) south flowing. Most of these rivers originate in the central part of the state where hill ranges are generally broader and higher. A northeast – southwest trending axis broadly marks the divide between the headwaters of north and south flowing rivers Fig.7. Continuity of such an axis, however, appears to have been disrupted by head ward erosion of streams that debouch a geologically susceptible terrain of recent origin.

The north flowing rivers form the part of the Barak river system of the neighboring Cachar plains of Assam. South flowing streams, on the other hand, form the part of the

Koladine river system of Myanmar. There are about 13 major streams of varying length (fig 7) in the state which owe their origin to the central highlands. North flowing R.Langkaih, Teirei, Tut and Tlawng (Dhaleswari), Serlui, Tuirial and Tuirini, Tuivawl and Tuivai form the sub systems of the Barak Valley.

South flowing rivers of Mat, Tuichang and Tuipui along with the border stream of Tiau belong to the larger Chhimtuipui (Koladine) system. However, the north flowing river Tuichawng of southern Mizoram along with its south flowing tributaries Kau and deh from the central highlands form the part of R.Karanphuli system that debouch the Chittagong Hill Tracts of Bangladesh in the west. These rivers occupy distinct basins clearly defined by the north – south alignment of the Hill ranges in the state (see fig 4)

Dranaiage Basin

Drainage basins are those units of landscape wherein system of streams contributes water to a network of stream channels. They are important topographic elements. Volume of discharge and intensity of surface flow influence the quality of land in a basin through denudation and deposition of detrital materials. Most landforms regardless of how they originate are modified by erosion and deposition associated with different patterns of running water. Drainage patterns are important particularly in humid areas because their development reflects rock type and geologic structure. Thus, analysis of drainage patterns is useful tool in geologic reconnaissance (Burchfiel et al., 1982:299-334). Stage(s) of gradation reflected in longitudinal and cross profile of rivers in a drainage basin shed considerable light upon its geologic history as well as indicate the influence of local geologic and climatic controls (Thornbury, 2002:100-111) - two variables that are believed to influence direction of area development and quality of human life immensely. It is in this light that the concept of watershed as a planning unit and its management was introduced in 1974 by the Ministry of Agriculture, Government of India. Initially, however, the scope

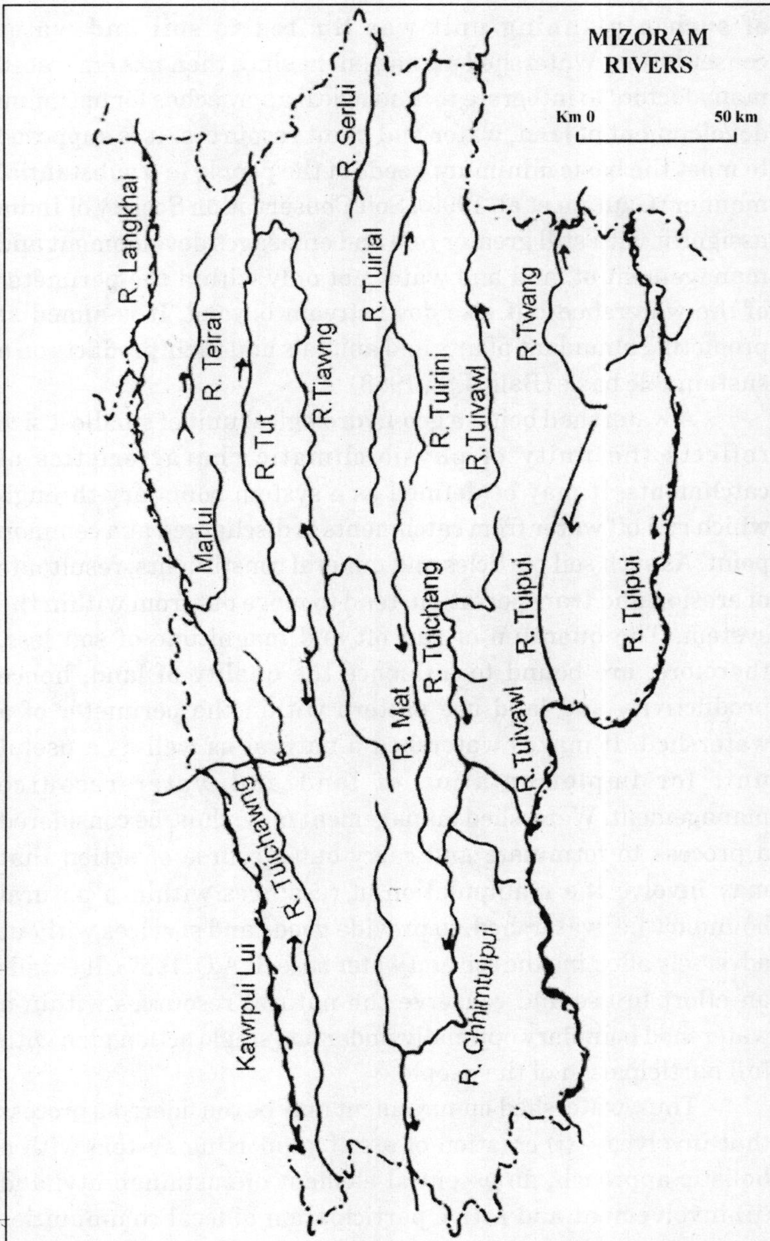
MIZORAM
RIVERS
Km 0
50 km
R. Langkhai
R. Teiral
R. Serlui
R. Tut
R. Tiawng
R. Tuirial
R. Tuirini
R. Tuivawl
R. Twang
Marlui
R. Tuichang
R. Mat
R. Tuipui
R. Tuipui
R. Tuivawl
R. Tuichawng
Kawrpui Lui
R. Chhimtuipui

Fig. 8

of such a planning unit was limited to soil and water conservation. Watershed management since then has embraced many factors to integrate technological approaches for optimum development of land, water and plant resources. It is supposed to meet the basic minimum needs of the people in a substantial manner (Gautam et al. 1995). Soil Conservation Society of India assigns it with still greater role and envisages development and management of land and water not only within the perimeter of the watershed but also downstream beyond. It is aimed at promoting abundant plants and animals and their products on a sustainable basis (Bali, J.S., 1988).

A watershed being a geo-hydrological unit of smallest size reflects the unity of physio-climatic characteristics of catchments. It may be defined as a system boundary through which run off water from catchments is discharged at a common point. As such soil particles and mineral constituents, resultants of erosion and transportation, tend to move out from within the system. The quantum of run off and magnitude of soil loss, therefore, are bound to influence the quality of land, hence productivity and land use pattern within the perimeter of a watershed. It makes watershed a natural as well as a useful unit for implementation of land and water resource management. Watershed management may, thus, be considered a process to formulate and carry out a course of action that may involve the manipulation of resources within a natural boundary i.e. watershed, to provide goods and services without adversely affecting the soil and water base (F.A.O, 1987). It entails an effort to use and conserve the natural resources within a watershed boundary optimally under one single action plan with full participation of the people.

Thus, watershed management may be considered a process that involves – (i) creation of a self supporting system with a holistic approach, an essential element of sustainability; and (ii) involvement and active participation of local communities in resource management, hence evolution of development plans from the grassroots levels. Such objectives presuppose man's innate urge to pave way for a sedentary living and bask in the security of a family and community life. As a matter of fact, the foundation of highest ideals of civilized societies have been laid down by the members of the communities which had had a relatively longer period of stability that sustained economic, political and social structures. A pre condition for such stability is the understanding of the interactive processes of which biotic and abiotic elements of nature are active agents. It is this interaction that has been shaping the culture of communities distinguishing one from the other for, the relationship of phenomena and its intensity vary spatially. It is the proper understanding of the significance of different phenomena in an interactive process with the knowledge of their tolerance limit (resilience) and accordant exploitation of resources for human consumption that may lead to sustainable resource utilization for men present and future. Man as an individual, in fact has a very short sighted view of things. He 'wants what he wants when he wants it' (Zimmermann, 1951). In the process, he does not care for the consequences. The communities are believed to curb individual's irrational urge to use resources. They are also believed to effectively moderate mans' greed hence unhampered exploitation of resources against the law of ecology and conservation. Generations of observations and experience of human communities are believed to have led to some understanding of the ecosystem it is part of. It is also supposed to make them selective in the use of innovations that present scientific world and technologies induce. It may go against the present day concept of high growth especially in the field of agriculture where new advances have been found to have adversely affected the land and water resources. As a result, agricultural operations on degrading land are becoming costlier and yields incompatible. The states of Punjab, Haryana, Andhra Pradesh, Gujarat and Maharashtra stand testimony to the plights of their farmers as they tried to harvest irrationally their land resources against the dictates of natural settings and principles of ecology.

It must also be realized that modern technological advances generally have led to uniform application of techniques and production strategies. It is not so much because innovations can not be adapted to unique situations. It is mostly due to ignorance of the people and lack of their comprehension about the ecosystem of the area where they are applied. As a result, the resilience of the ecosystem is generally surpassed disturbing the homoeostasis. There are innumerable examples the world over that the basic resources that mankind is beholden to for his own survival, has been irreparably damaged rendering the regions unsustainable as the cost of its repair, even if possible, may be prohibitive under existing economies of scale. Realization, however, is growing to identify the tolerance limit of the systems (Singh, 2003). And as stated earlier ecosystem units may be identified with watersheds or catchments for, they represent uniqueness of the interlinkage amongst the biotic and abiotic elements consequent upon the unity of physico-climatic characteristics. Moreover, watershed may unambiguously be defined from topographic maps and may easily be broken, as Haggett (1961) observed, into a 'hierarchic system of smaller basins' which will fit exactly in the next larger basin. Not only this, if the land and its productivity have not been tempered with injudicious application of technological innovations the vegetal cover and catena will reflect a correspondence that sustain energy flow hence ecosystem in a particular watershed. This requires an understanding of distribution of climatic energy in conjunction with the terrestrial attributes of different regions.

WATERSHEDS OF MIZORAM

In Mizoram, as suggested by the Institute of Resource Development and Social Management (IRDAS), Hydrabad (Anon. 1994), 22 distinct watersheds may easily be identified (Fig.9).

The Institute made an exhaustive study of all the watersheds taking into account geomorphic parameters that apparently influence watershed shape, drainage pattern, and

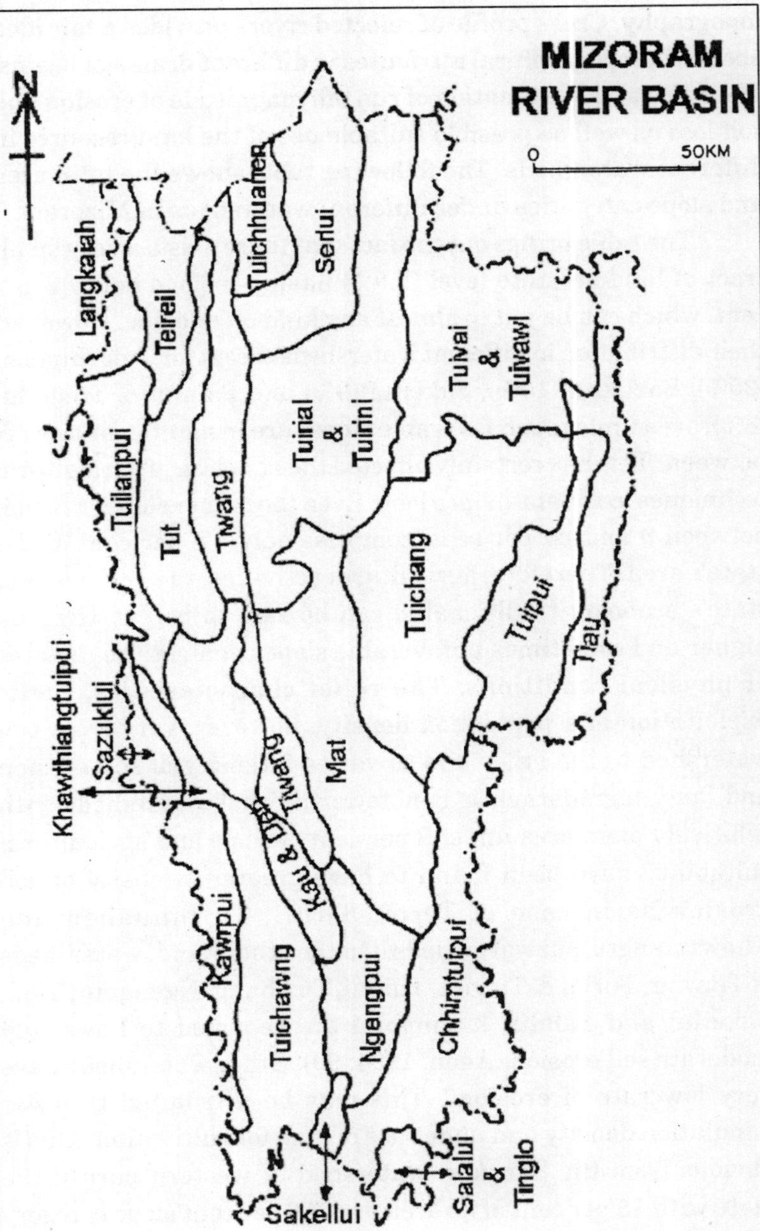
MIZORAM
RIVER BASIN
0
50KM
N
Langkaiah
Teireil
Tuichhuahen
Serlui
Tuilanpui
Tut
Twang
Tuinal
&
Tuirini
Tuivai
&
Tuivawl
Tuichang
Tuipui
Tiau
Khawthiangtuipui
Sazuklui
Twang
Mat
Kau & Dah
Kawrpui
Tuichawng
Ngengpui
Chhimtuipui
Sakellui
Salalui
&
Tinglo

Fig. 9

topography. Cross profile of selected rivers provides a fair idea about the topographical attributes in different drainage basins. They also allow estimation of run off, magnitude of erosion and soil loss as well as possible suitable use of the land resource in different watersheds. The following table shows the total area and slope categories under different watersheds in Mizoram.

The table brings out the fact that there exists a very small tract of land on state level (2.9%) having a slope below 8 per cent, which can be put to almost any kind of land use. However, their distribution in different watersheds except for Tuichhuahen (25%), Sazuklui (15%), Sakeilui (9%) and Salalui & Tingo lui (8%), area under such favorable slopes are insignificant and far between. This has certainly affected the adoption of agricultural techniques in the state since long. Even the higher slopes ranging between 9 and 20 per cent, comprise only 4.8 per cent of the state's area. Therefore, agricultural activities, the very basis of state's economy traditionally, can be said to be practiced on higher and sometimes unfavorable slopes against the dictates of physical conditions. The relief characteristics, biotic exploitation and population density, however, vary from one watershed to the other and so varies intensity of soil erosion and land degradation. It is noteworthy that watersheds with relatively more area under 8 per cent of slope and agricultural suitability have been found to have greater intensity of soil erosion as in case of Terei, Serlui, Tuichhuahen and Khawthlangtuipui watersheds. On the other hand, watersheds of Tlawng, Turial & Tuirini, Tuipui, Tuichang, Ngengpui, Tiau, Sakeilui and Salalui & Tingolui are reported to have only moderate soil erosion (Anon. 1994: 99). Other watersheds have very low rate of erosion. This may be attributed to lower population density and under use of land for cultivation. This is obvious from the Sazuklui watershed in western part of the state with 15 per cent of its area under 8 per cent slope category being rated as having low intensity of soil erosion. This also is indicative of the fact that there still exists a scope for agricultural

TABLE – 1:1*

Distribution of Slopes Under Different Watersheds in Mizoram

Sl. No	*Name of Watershed*	*Area (in hect.)*	*Percent (state area)*	*Categories of slope in %(area in hectares)*			
				<8	*9-20*	*21-50*	*>50*
1.	Langkaiah	39464	1.87	2368	2369	16574	8153
2.	Teirei	67828	3.22	3394	2034	43409	67828
3.	Tut	83629	3.97	3345	3345	51850	25089
4.	Tlawng	170145	8.07	3403	8507	85073	73162
5.	Serlui	64717	3.07	3236	2589	29122	29770
6.	Tuichhuahen	26071	1.29	6518	782	11731	7040
7.	Tuirial & Tuirini	179527	8.51	1795	3590	12387	50268
8.	Tuivai & Tuivawl	230977	10.95	2310	11549	18478	19864
9.	Mat	96390	4.57	3856	9639	36620	46267
10.	Tuipui	87933	4.17	2638	879	51881	32535
11.	Tuichang	16009	7.59	1601	3202	137685	17611

(Contd.)

(Contd. Table 1.1)

Sl. No	Name of Watershed	Area (in hect.)	Percent (state area)	Categories of slope in %(area in hectares) <8	9-20	21-50	>50
12.	Ngengpui	71179	3.38	1425	4270	29183	36301
13.	Tuilianpui	12703	6.02	2541	7620	57157	59691
14.	Sazuklui	11561	0.55	1734	2312	3700	3815
15.	Khawthlangpui	14901	0.71	894	447	9387	4173
16.	Kau & Deh	97718	4.67	2931	2931	7818	84038
17.	Tuichawng	12752	6.05	2552	10207	51033	63790
18.	Kawrpui	35620	1.69	3205	8193	16029	8193
19.	Chhimtuipui	27405	13.00	5481	5481	35628	227465
20.	Tiau	87526	4.15	1750	1751	25382	58643
21.	Sakeilui	25585	1.21	2303	5884	9723	7675
22.	Salalui & Tingolui	28989	1.37	2319	4058	10436	28989
	Mizoram	21089	100	61599	101639	863515	1081736

**Adopted from IRDAS Report (1994) on Soil Erosion and Land Degradation problem in Mizoram.*

colonization if the activity is diffused to less crowded watersheds in accordance with their physical and ecological conditions. This may also reduce further degradation of watersheds where problem appears to be grave.

Climate

Climate is probably the most important factor of all geographical influences affecting man. The potential economic activity, particularly crop producing ability, of a given area is dependent primarily upon the existing climatic and soil conditions. climatic factors exert mainly a regional influence on plant life, the difference in the behaviour of a crop or group of crops over extensive area, as in given state or group of states may be considered due primarily to difference in climatic condition (Klages, 1958).

Mizoram generally enjoys a subtropical climate of monsoon type. The temperature conditions, however, are moderated due to altitudinal variations and alignment of the hill ranges. They are markedly different than areas on same latitudes in central India. Two distinct seasons may be recognized in Mizoram, one with abundance of rainfall extending generally from later part of April to the early part of October and the other, almost a dry period from October to March interspersed with uncertain cyclonic rains associated with north eastern monsoon during winter months and cyclonic disturbance in south east Asia before the on set of south west monsoon. An additional characteristic of rainfall in the state is the continuity of pre monsoon rain with that of south west monsoon rains that breaks generally along the Bengal Coast by 14th June. The phenomena though not yet fully comprehended may have to do with the northward movement of jet stream that establishes itself just south of the Himalayas in lower stratosphere by May and results in northward expansion of ITCZ (Inter Tropical Convergence Zone) with associated disturbances in the lower troposphere.

The influence of jet stream on the on set of south west monsoon over Indian subcontinent is heralded by its sudden shift to Tibetan highland. It results in the burst of monsoon in most parts of India with significant dry spells in between. But the western pacific cyclonic movement caused by the northward movement of the ITCZ results in rains over South East Asia before the break of monsoon in India. The NE states including Mizoram comes under its influence that causes pre-monsoon rains to continue without break till the south western monsoon overtakes this region. The spatial and temporal occurrence of rain, is, however, guided by the pressure gradient over the Pacific influenced by the relative strength of El Nino and La Nino off the coast of Peru. Thus, the pre-monsoon and monsoon rains in these parts appear to be closely related with the atmospheric as well as oceanic oscillations over the Indian sub continent and the Pacific Ocean respectively. The relief features of north eastern parts of the country also plays a significant role in arresting moisture laden pre-monsoon cyclonic rains caused by the interplay between the jet stream and the ITCZ that are independent of the normal planetary wind system over these parts. By the middle of September the position of jet stream and ITCZ starts getting reversed with apparent southward shift of the sun. The atmospheric and oceanic circulations assume the conditions similar to that of pre-monsoon period. Thus, with the withdrawal of south west monsoon cyclonic disturbances bring about rain in NE India almost in continuous succession. It extends the rainy season in these parts for more than two months in comparison to northern and central India.

Weather Condition

As is obvious the weather conditions do not vary much except for the two distinct seasons – (a) prolonged rainy season from April to mid-October and (b) dry period from mid-October to March. The seasons broadly correspond with summer and winter. The weather elements vary with little magnitude in

Mizoram. The period corresponding to spring in other parts of the country i.e. February to March is marked with bright sunshine, rising temperature and speedy winds. The period is also marked with low relative humidity in the state. The temperature in this pre rain season generally fluctuates between 18°C to 23°C.

During rainy months, corresponding generally with the summer in the north Indian plains, temperature ranges from 21°C to 33°C though in previous 2-3 years temperature above 35°C have been recorded. Post rainy season period is marked with a temperature variation between 18°C to 25°C and moderately high velocity winds. Temperature declines further in winter to 11°C to 21°C. The relative humidity in the aftermath of the rainy season is soon lowered due to terrestrial attributes and vegetal cover. The springs and cataracts are replenished and provide the people respite from the problem of water shortage. In pre rain months of February and March these springs are exhausted. The people have to face difficulty even in managing their household chores. Unavailability of a regular source of sufficient water may be one of the reasons which might have discouraged the local farmers to adopt farming of rabi crops on any significant scale. Even rivers which swell during the rainy season shrivel during this period.

Except for these fluctuations the temperature condition in the state remains generally pleasant. The annual range of temperature is generally below 20°C. The winters are cool and summers at its height only warm. The state never experiences cold waves of winter or hot waves of summer that overtake most part of north Indian plains and take thousand of lives every year. Such a weather condition may be exploited to encourage tourism and associated industries in the state. They may provide the people an alternative and gainful employment option.

As stated earlier, the state appears to be experiencing rise in temperature the cause of which is difficult to establish as data on temperature and humidity are few and far between to suggest any trend. There, however, may be many factors or combination of factors that may be responsible for such warming. Simplistically the temperature rise in the state is attributed to large scale deforestation and jhum cultivation. But this may also be affected by climatic change that is overtaking the globe as a whole or to 12 years cycle of solar eruptions which was recorded nearest to the earth in 2005 and may be the cause of recent warming at least partially. There, however, is no doubt that denudation of vegetal cover and up surge in concrete based structures combined with rise in the number and magnitude of vehicular movement must be responsible for affecting thermal structure of atmosphere locally.

Distribution of Rainfall

As is obvious, the weather characteristic in Mizoram is dominated not as much by temperature parameters as by quantum of rain fall (or absence of it) in its spatial and temporal dimensions. The state on an average receives over 250 cm. of annual rainfall of which over 95% is received only during the long rainy season. This makes the winter months really dry in the state.

There is also a marked variation in spatial distribution of rainfall in the state. The area just south of central highlands receives the highest amount of rainfall. The western and north western parts of the state though receive a very high amount of rainfall (over 250 cm) the magnitude is strikingly low when compared to central Mizoram Fig. 10. Similarly, the Lurh – Phawngpui Range and their western slopes also receive over 250 cm of rainfall but lower than the central parts of the state. The same trend continues south ward where the valley between the higher Phawngpui range and the rolling hills of the south western Mizoram receives the highest amount of rain fall. This obviously suggests that the alignment of the hills in the state has a definite bearing on rainfall distribution and the rain shadow effect exerted by these ranges cause significant spatial variability in the magnitude of rainfall. It is most revealing in the eastern parts between the Kawnpui – Aizawl – Hmuifang range in the west and the Chalfilh – Tawi – Lurh ranges in the east covering a very large area of Champhai district. Apparently the rain shadow effects of central ranges cause lesser quantity of rain in this agriculturally important area. However, during rainy season the variability has little significance as no part of the state receives rain fall less than 200 cm. During winter months, conversely, no area receives more than 4 cm. of rain on an average and suffers from dry condition. The worst affected area is the south eastern part – the western slopes of the Phawngpui range.

On the basis of magnitude of rainfall and thermal characteristics the state may be divided in two climatic regions. On the basis of scheme suggested by R.L. Singh (1971): (a) very humid central part of Mizoram having over 300cm of rainfall with summer and winter temperature having a variation of 21°C to 33°C and 11°C to 21°C respectively, and (b) humid to sub- humid slopes of the Sialkal – Hrangturzo range in the east where annual rain fall is recorded between 100 and 200 cm. Similarly, the areas along the western boundary particularly west of the Reiek range experiences relatively lesser rain fall where it varies between 200 and 300 cm. In respect of temperature, however, all parts of the state have almost identical conditions.

Thus, the most characteristic features of the climate of Mizoram are found in excessiveness, diffusion, seasonal variability and unreliability of rainfall which for domestic and agricultural consumptions are the most meaningful. As the rainfall conditions are dominated by monsoon primarily and depressions secondarily the farmers are guided by them in their choice of enterprises. For example, in the eastern, north eastern and extreme southern parts he always avoids climatically sensitive enterprises particularly on higher altitudes. The alignment of hill ranges has considerable influence on the rainfall condition. At the same time, high altitude with its vegetal cover modifying temperature conditions reduces loss of moisture in

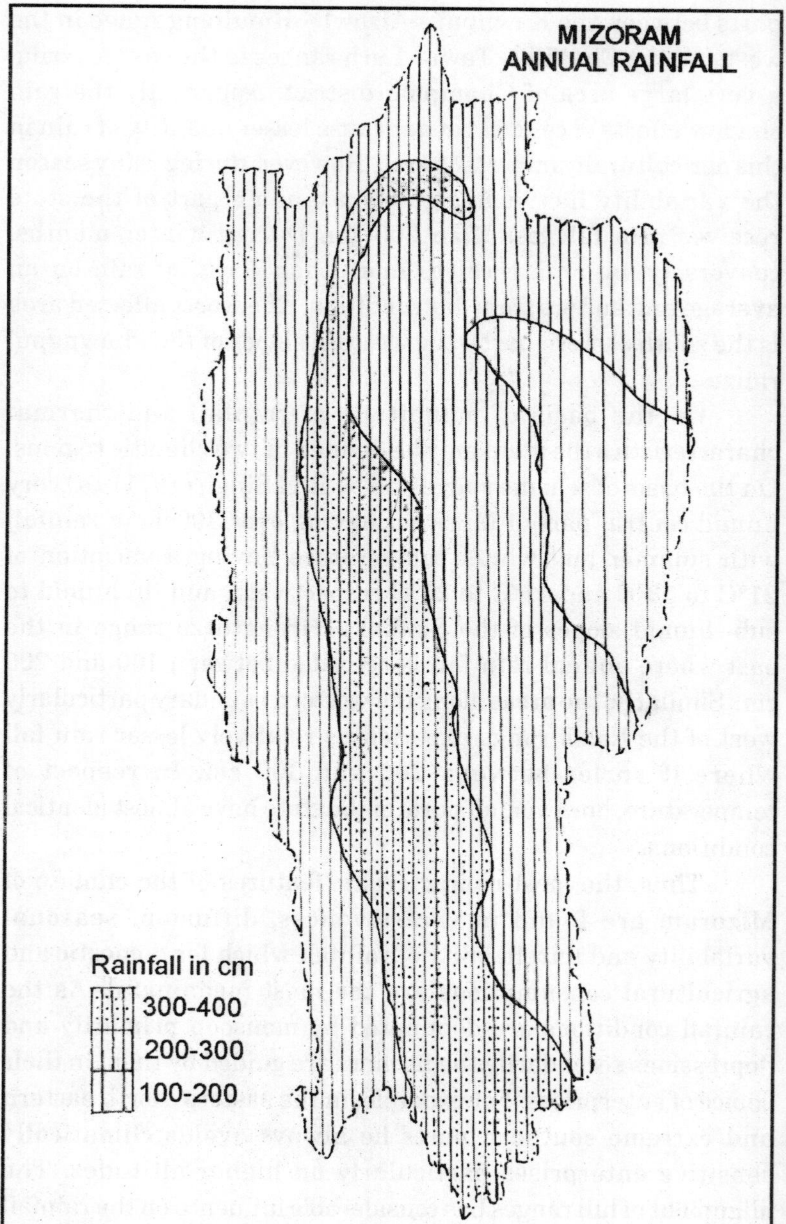
MIZORAM
ANNUAL RAINFALL
Rainfall in cm
300-400
200-300
100-200

Fig. 10 (a)

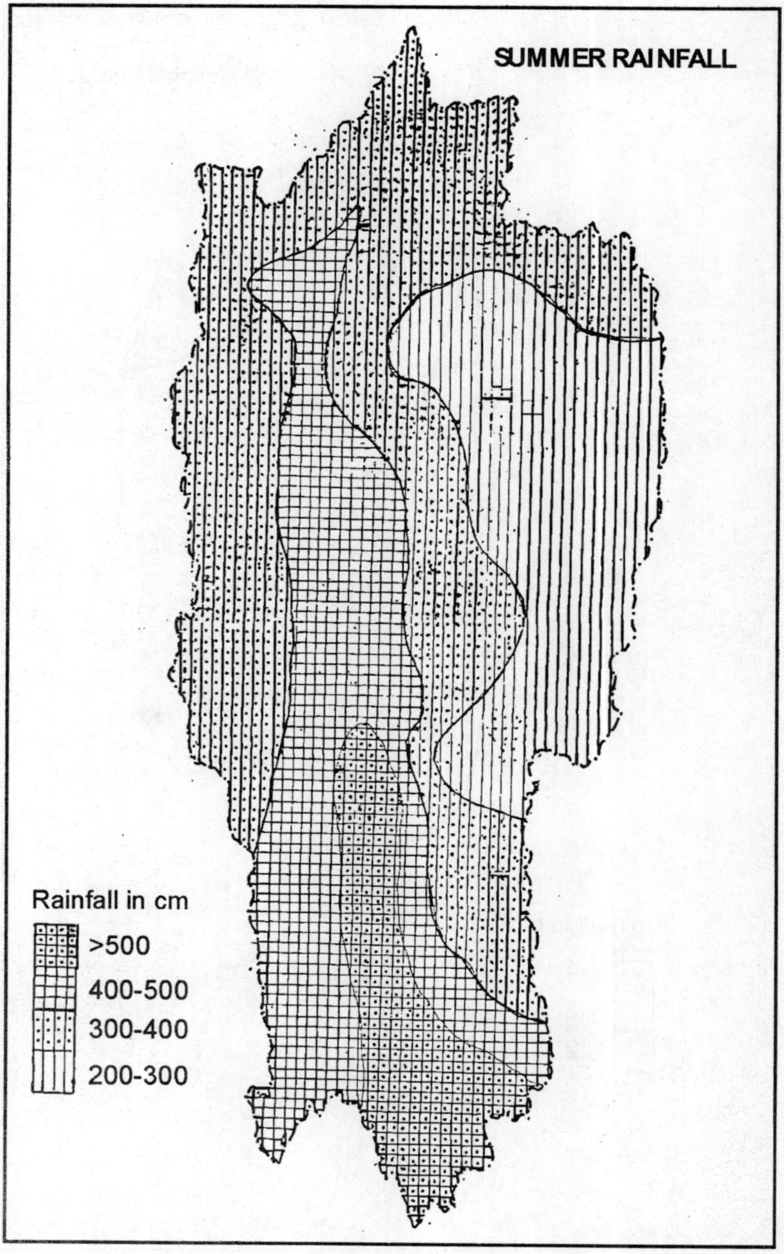

Fig. 10 (b)

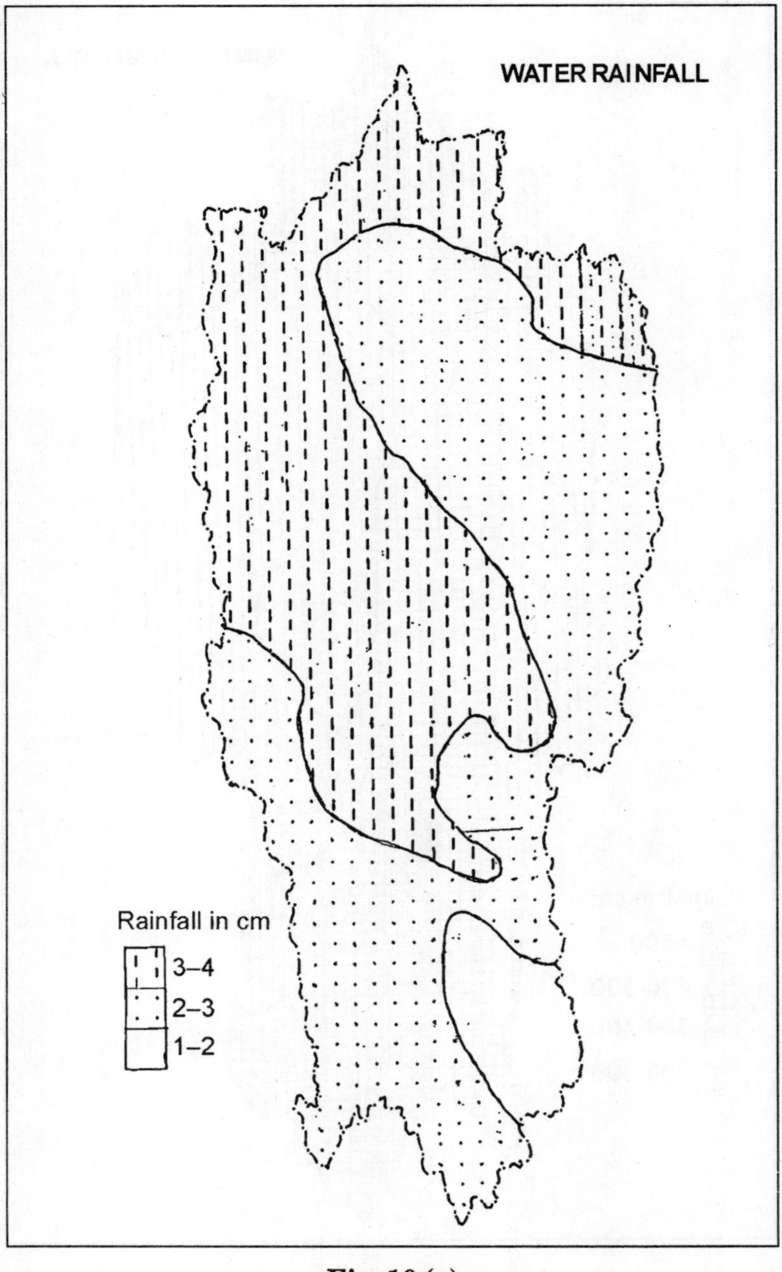

Fig. 10 (c)

most area. But it is significant to note that annual range of temperature is moderately high and combined with the terrain attributes and soil profile it becomes very significant in the agricultural economy of the state. The summer temperatures which are considerably high enable the farmers to grow Kharif crops in the main.

Rainfall and temperature parameters are, though, the most important indicators of regional differences in climatic conditions, considering the extensive areas under vegetative cover in the state potential evapotranspiration (PE) becomes a very critical element of climatic resource, firstly because it includes the spatial analysis of rainfall and temperature conditions and secondly, because the influence of vegetation and soil is also taken into account in its calculation. As a matter of fact, a simple analysis of rainfall and temperature conditions is not of much significance unless it is correlated with regional economy. As PE is considered to have a more significant impact on the agricultural economy it requires to be evaluated as a critical parameter in a predominantly agrarian state.

Potential evapotranspiration refers to the maximum amount of water that could be evaporated from vegetation and land surface assuming an unlimited moisture supply in the ground (Singh, 1971). The dependent factors in agricultural problems concern those which are related to the sub moisture content, the ease of movement of water through the soil profile and the depth of ground water. These properties to large extent, determine the potentials for crop combinations. Thornthwait's (1948) water balance procedure takes this into account. As spatial and temporal characteristics of precipitation affect moisture on the one hand and the amount of PE and saturation of the soil on the other, water surplus or deficit occurs in different areas. Hence, a comparison of PE and precipitation and their percentage variation become significant. It also provides convincing explanation of vegetative growth and cropping pattern.

In an agricultural state like Mizoram though assessment of PE is necessary it is difficult to be calculated as required data on temperature are not available at micro regional level. The soil, with an adequate vegetation cover, however, should always be at field capacity. Since the condition is maintained in most part of the state, the optimum level PE is obtained in general. The moisture supplies from rainfall, soil moisture and soil moisture storage usually exceed over the PE during rainy months. The soil moisture, however, is quickly depleted and limits farmer in their choice of agricultural enterprise with the on set of winter.

Soils

Soils in common parlance refer to the earth material that are modified by the interaction of physical, chemical and biological processes to enable them to perform three basic functions:

(a) to act as a physical support to vegetation
(b) to serve as a medium for storing water and bringing it into contact with rooted plants, and
(c) to supply a small but essential percentage of nutrients which are converted into plant food.

This necessarily suggests that soils consist of different types of material that include weathered rock, organic material water and various gases in the form of air. It is the proportion of these materials that leads to the variations in the nutrients hence fertility of the soils. The proportion of these materials is influenced by climate, topography, geology and nature and extent of vegetation (Burchfield, et.al. 1982).

Geologically soils may be classified on the basis of the materials upon which soils form. Weathering being the first step in the process of soil formation, the weathered earth materials may remain 'in situ' with their modifications induced by organic processes. Such soils are termed as 'residual' as the pedalfer of the Peninsular India. Such soils are almost non existent in Mizoram. On the other hand, if the transport of the parent materials is induced by the sub aerial agents of erosion, which may include Aeolian, fluvial or glacial processes and modification of their characteristics through weathering and organic processes at the place where they are moved to, lead to classification of soils as transported. Most of the fertile soil of flood plains of the world and soils of glacial deposits of mid latitudes or loess of temperate deserts provide the example of transported soils. Similarly, the river valleys in the state have relative abundance of transported soils. The soils on hill slopes, however, show characteristics of leaching and erosion and may be considered independent of the two types – unexploited and protected. Exploitation can mean soil destruction and depletion through erosion and overuse. Population growth, increasing pressure on land and somewhat modern farm technology are bringing about a breakdown in the traditional system of dry farming and fallowing in the state. By the improvement of agricultural water supply (wherever feasible), use of chemical fertilizer and high yielding exotic seeds, the period of fallowing is being shortened and the intensity of cropping is increasing. There appears to be a thrust on terracing of cultivable land on fragile slopes. It is an attempt to defy the geophysical processes at enormous ecological and economic cost - all because the government and the farmers are swayed by the uniform application of technology and accordant production of crops. Little is realized that improved farming technology may be used in accordance with the terrain and soil attributes to increase the productivity of indigenous and suitable crops. There also exists ample scope for the expansion of cultivation which may be achieved by agricultural colonization of the cultivable wasteland on various slope categories. Judicious use of its soil resources becomes all the more significant in Mizoram as land degradation is accentuated by a heavy rainfall and shortening jhum cycle. The attempt to increase the productivity of the land through terracing of the slopes is no less injurious. It may enhance soil erosion as the slopes will have to adjust to new levels. In the process soil erosion may be accelerated and exceed traditional tilling in which at least some measures are taken to reduce the degradation of cultivable slopes.

Soils in Mizoram vary according to altitude. On ridge tops soils generally exhibit organic matter with heavy and coarse texture varying from high to medium. Lower slopes have shallow texture and scanty profile development. On the other hand, at the foot of the slopes, the soils are generally poor and light and contain low organic matter with increasing amount of silt and sand.

Soils are generally acidic and rich in organic matters which make them nitrogen rich. However, potash and phosphorus contents are low and need to be supplemented according to the requirements of the crops. River valleys are endowed with transported soil from the upslope with heavy textures but low profile development. The soils of the state are generally argillaceous on lower slopes and the valleys. They are arnaceous on ridge tops and higher altitudes. The soils are highly leached due to excessive rain and consequent slope wash.

National Bureau of Soil Survey and Land Use Planning, ICAR, Nagpur; with cooperation of agriculuture department, Gov't of Mizoram (2000) has made a very detailed survey of the soils of Mizoram It classified them in 31 sub groups under four major topo-geologic formations: (a) Soils of Purvanchal Hill Range; (b) Soils of Narrow Valleys; (c) Soil of Purvanchal Hills; and (d) Soils of Surma Valleys. These topo units exhibit a wide range of soil groups which vary in their texture, moisture retention capacity and aeration. They may be classified under 10 major soil families of Hapludalfs; Hapahldults; Peleudults; Dystrochrepts; Hoplohumults; Dystochrepts; Kanhapludalfs, Palendalfs; Fluvaquents and Udifluents. Five major soil types of the ten families are shown in Fig. 11.

Soils of these families vary in texture, aeration, and drainage characteristics according to the altitude and nature of slopes they occupy. On the basis of their texture, however, the soils of Mizoram may broadly be classified in five categories:

(i) Loamy Skeletal Soil (ii) Coarse Loam
(iii) Fine Loam (iv) Silt Soil
(v) Clayey Fine Soil

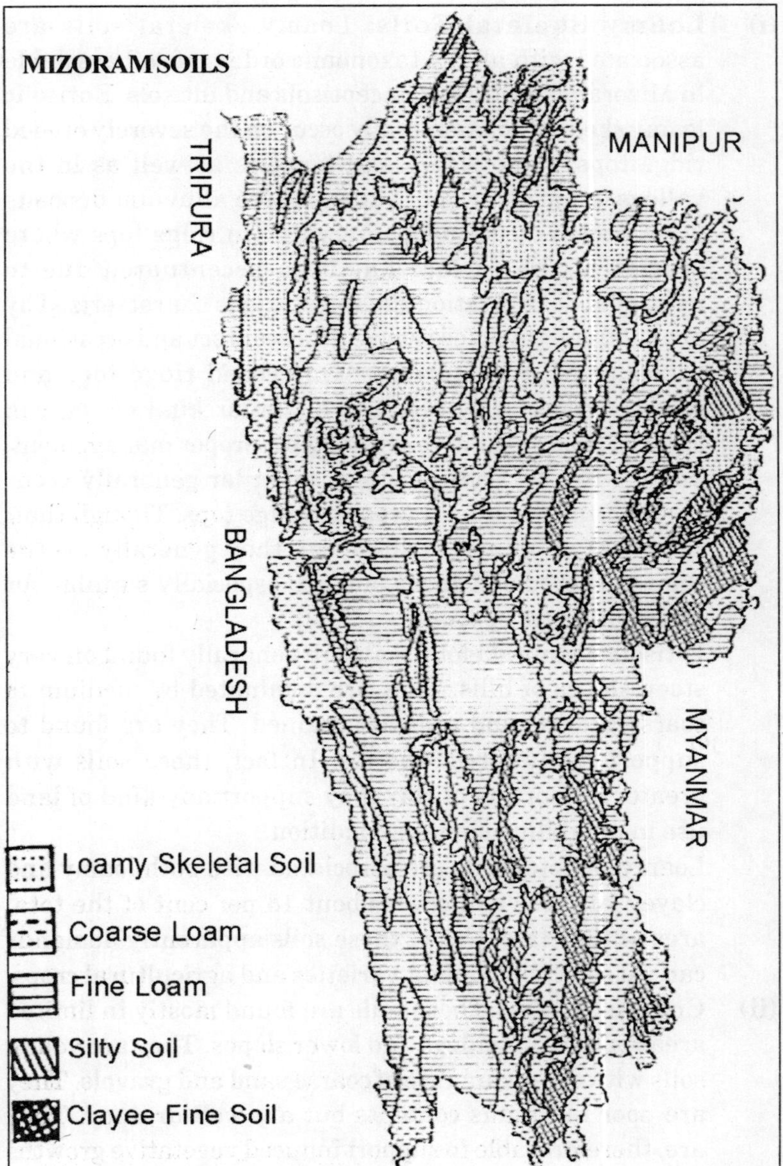
MIZORAM SOILS
MANIPUR
TRIPURA
BANGLADESH
MYANMAR
Loamy Skeletal Soil
Coarse Loam
Fine Loam
Silty Soil
Clayee Fine Soil
5 0 5 10 15 20 25 Km
MYANMAR

Fig. 11

(i) **Loamy Skeletal Soils:** Loamy skeletal soils are associated with all the taxonomic orders of soil available in Mizoram i.e. entisols, inceptisols and ultisols. Entisolic loamy skeletal soils generally occur on the severely eroded ridge tops, steep slopes and terraces as well as in the valleys of narrow river courses where alluvium deposits are common at frequent intervals. On ridge tops where erosion of the surface has been accentuated due to irrational deforestation the soil strata is characterized by about 50 cm. thickness above lithic contact and occasional exposure of rock surfaces. On eroded ridge tops and terraces covered with scrubs a similar kind of soil can support good vegetative growth with proper management. Loamy skeletal soils of inceptisol order generally occur in sub-humid to humid areas on ridge tops. Though their thickness is limited to 40-50 cm. they generally overlie the weathered soft rocks and are especially suitable for different forest species.

Ultisolic loamy skeletal soils are generally found on very steep slopes of hills. They are dominated by medium to coarse gravels and are well drained. They are found to support many forest species. In fact, these soils with greater proportion of clay may support any kind of land use in prevailing climatic condition.

Loamy skeletal soils are associated with both loamy and clayey surfaces and cover about 18 per cent of the total area of the state. Use of these soils apparently demands careful selection of plant varieties and agricultural crops.

(ii) **Coarse Loam:** These soils are found mostly in limited areas of narrow valleys and lower slopes. They are young soils with the dominance of coarse sand and gravels. They are poor in humus contents but are well drained. They are, therefore, able to support induced vegetative growths for few years. It may be this reason that these soils have long been used for jhum cultivation in the state. These soils occupy about 23 per cent of the total area and are significant in the agricultural economy of the state.

(iii) **Fine Loam:** Fine loams are the most widespread soil type in the state. It covers over 48 per cent of the total area of the state. However, fine loams of inceptisol order which occupy steep slopes of narrow river valleys and terraces are generally poor in carbonates.

Fine loams of ultisol order classified as aqults are found in patches of flat lands. With argillic character they are not so well drained but are used presently for rice cultivation in the state. Humult ultisols, on the other hand, are never saturated with water and are rich in organic carbon in the upper argillic horizon. They dominate on steep to very steep slopes and are rich in humus contents. Good soil drainage and fertility support good forest growth.

Besides, fine loamy well-drained udult soils occur very widely on very steep side of slopes. They are also found on flat lands and represent the type of soils, which may be formed in the physiographic and climatic conditions obtained in Mizoram. But they are generally poor in humus content and require replenishing of nutrients after they are used for 3-4 years.

(iv) **Silt Soil :** Silt dominated soils in Mizoram generally occur in the river basins of R. Tiau and R. Tuipui in the eastern part of the state. They are also found in small-elongated patches along R. Mat and R. Chhimpuitui in southern Mizoram. They occupy only about 4 per cent of the total area. They are moderately deep and imperfectly drained. They generally occupy eroded side slopes of the hills and may have fine to coarse texture depending on the steepness of the slopes. However, almost 50 per cent these soils are coarse silt on nearly level valleys and support thick vegetative growth.

(v) **Clayey Fine Soils:** These soils are obtained mostly on steep to very steep slopes with severe erosion and clayey surface. They are mostly found in eastern and southern parts of the state. They are usually deep and well drained with fine texture on ridge tops. They account for 7 per cent of the total area of the state in different patches and are significant natural resource that may help improve the agricultural economy of the state.

Natural Vegetation

Natural vegetation is the reflection of physio-climatic and soil characteristics of a region (Warming, 1909; Raunkiar, 1934). They represent the 'biotic response' that exhibits variations in the 'a biotic' environment and suggest the potential productive uses of the area that may form the nuclei of human settlements and their activities (Haggett, 1983:89-90). As a renewable resource they directly or indirectly provide sustenance to the people who depend on it. They are also instrumental in regulating the geo-bio-chemical and hydrological cycles hence recharge of groundwater, maintenance of nutrients in soil and life sustaining gases in the atmosphere. Forests are believed to absorb 65 tons of co_2 per hectare; release 3.5 to 5 tons of photosynthetic oxygen. It is estimated that due to loss of tropical forests alone there is 10 to 30 per cent of co_2 in atmosphere. They also act as biological filter that sieves dust and industrial pollutants that may find their way to the atmosphere. It is suggested that one hectare of proper vegetal cover filters about 30-35 tons of dust generated to atmosphere. A 1984 study came to the conclusion that about one billion cubic meters of oxygen was being replaced by co_2 every year due to deforestation. They also act as sinks to hazardous atmospheric gases. Thinning of vegetal cover of the earth is one of the major reasons for increasing amount of Green House Gases in the atmosphere leading to global warming and is likely to raise the temperature between 1.5 °C and 4.5 °C by the year 2030.

They themselves are invaluable resource. They are also indicative of the direction that man's farming activities ought to take (Huntington, 1951:421). They also exhibit a pattern that develops in response to evolutionary processes encompassing environmental changes (Kellman, 1975). In general, vegetations reflect the environmental factors that set a broad limit for the range of plant species – actual and potential, and their productivity (Paterson, 1956: 142-45) through their combinations and interactions.

In fact, environment of any organism including the plants represents the sum of the interactive phenomena that enter its system and activates its metabolism. Reactions favorable to the demand of ontogeny allow them to flourish in similar conditions. Unfavorable conditions, on the other hand, may affect morphological and genetic attributes adversely and smother them (Mason & Langenheim, 1957: 325-40) as their tolerance limit is exceeded. Although the impact of individual ecological factors may be isolated, generally there may be many elements, it may be noted, that may lead to 'non-resource' effects impinging on colonization of plants. In a small state like that of Mizoram, however, many of the climatic as well as edaphic factors may be difficult to be segregated. Yet, some factors like moisture supply, altitude and direction of the slopes stand out in differentiating the types of vegetation in different parts of the state.

The state of Mizoram is well endowed with a vegetative cover ranging from tropical wet evergreen to montane sub-tropical alpine type. The terrain and climatic attributes provide it with large potential for forest growth and its development. But increasing population pressure, extensive practice of jhum cultivation and its reducing cycle, unhindered domestic and commercial exploitation for timber, bamboo and fuel wood are some reasons depleting the the state of its forest cover. It appears to have adversely affected the water recharge mechanism. It is paradoxical in an area receiving over 250 cm. of rainfall every year and suffering from shortage of water year after year. And though there are no reliable data available it shows in early drying of springs that used to sustain the settlements as late as early part of March. More often than not, such springs are found to dry by the end of December.

Area under forests in Mizoram is reported to be 16717 sq. km. i.e. about 79 per cent of its total geographical area. Out of this, 67 per cent is classified as open forest (FSI, 2003). The survey further suggests that only 23 per cent of the forested area may be classified as having dense forest. It is estimated that about 40,000 to 50,000 hectares of forested land is brought under jhum cultivation every year. It results in a loss of about 1.25 per cent of the vegetative cover. Due to reduction in the period of jhum cycle, these areas are unable to regenerate plants in real terms. Even notified forests (reserved and protected), which account for over 68 per cent of the total forest area and over 54 per cent of the geographical area, are no exception. About 18 per cent of these forests have also been degraded and may be having a canopy cover of less than 10 per cent. Rest of the forests are administered either by the District Councils or Village Councils. Degradation of forests has significantly brought down the revenue generated from forests to Rs.125

TABLE: 1:2
Different Categories of Forests in Mizoram
(Area in sq. km)

Forests	*1994-95*	*2002-03*
Reserved	5509	7909
Protected	1647	3568
Unclassed	3589	5240
Total forests	10745#	16717 *

Source: # Statistical Hand Book Mizoram 1996, Directorate of Economics and Statistics, Govt. of Mizoram.
*Forest Survey of India, 2003, State of Forest Report 2003, MoEE, Government of India.

TABLE: 1:3

Districtwise Distribution of Forests in Mizoram

Districts	*Area (in km^2) forest*	*Dense forests*	*Open forests*	*Total forest*	*Area under forests (in per cent)*
Aizawl	3576	665	2317	1982	83.9
Champhai	3186	592	2042	633	82.1
Mamit	3026	562	1929	2490	82.5
Serchhip	1422	264	800	1069	74.2
Kolasib	1383	257	769	1028	74.0
Lunglei	4538	706	3065	3775	83.3
Lawngtlai	1991	371	1015	1384	69.6
Saiha	1966	368	995	1362	69.2
Mizoram	21087	3786	12931	16717	79.28

lakh in 1999-2000 from about 156 lakh in 1994-95, despite the fact that the area under forests has increased by about 56 per cent from 10745 sq. km. in 1994-95 to 16717 sq. km in 2002-03 .

The following table shows area under different category of forests in Mizoram in 1994-95 and 2002 03.

An analysis of the distribution of forests at district level brings forth the fact that the districts dominated by rural population are also the districts which have lower proportion of forest. It may be attributed to the changes introduced with regard to agriculture in last 20 years in order to discourage people from undertaking jhum cultivation. In addition, creation of new districts in 1998 also appears to have adversely affected the forest areas in the state. The following table shows district wise distribution of different classes of forests.

Distribution of area under forests on district level also appears to have been affected by growing concentration of population in urban centers. Districts with larger proportion of urban population (generally proportional to the significance of the towns) also have larger areas under forests. Thus, the districts of Aizawl with four major townships, Champhai with five, Lunglei and Mamit with three each have over 82 per cent of area under forests. This may also be attributed to the fact that most of the reserved forests with wild life sanctuaries are located in these northern districts of the state, On the other hand, the districts with smaller areas but more number of towns have much less area under forest as in case of the districts of Kolasib and Serchip with four and three townships respectively (forest area about 74 per cent). Predominantly rural districts of Saiha and Lawngtlai have forest areas around 69 per cent, much below the state average.

Based on the topographical attributes and climatic variations the forests of Mizoram has been classified in three broad categories as:

(1) Tropical Wet Evergreen Forests

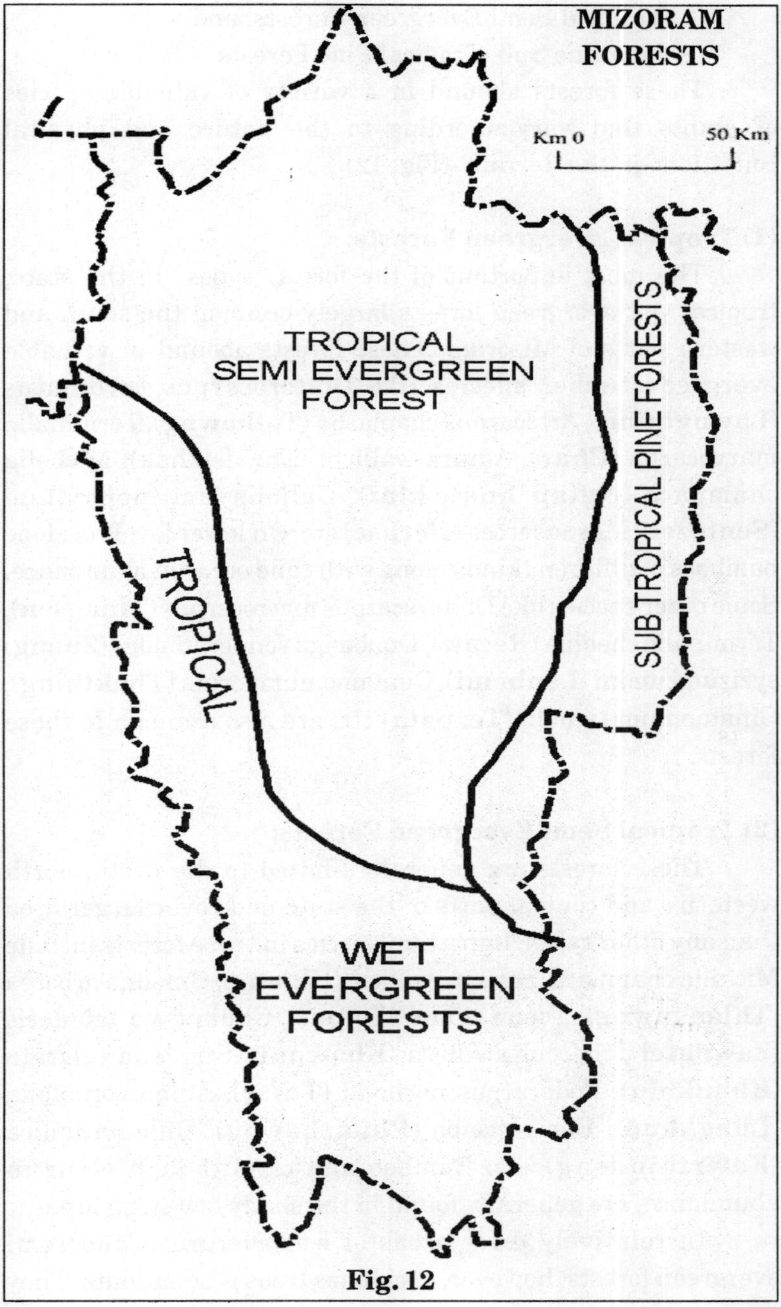
MIZORAM
FORESTS
Km 0
50 Km
TROPICAL
SEMI EVERGREEN
FOREST
SUB TROPICAL PINE FORESTS
TROPICAL
WET
EVERGREEN
FORESTS

Fig. 12

(2) Tropical Semi Evergreen Forests, and

(3) Montane Sub- Tropical Pine Forests

These forests abound in a variety of valuable species of plants that vary according to the nature and physical condition of the terrain (Fig. 12).

(1) Tropical Evergreen Forests:

The most important of the forest types in the state, tropical wet evergreen forests largely occur in the south and western parts of Mizoram. These forests abound in valuable evergreen timber species like Dipterocarpus turbinatus (**Lawngthing**), Artocarpus chaplasha (**Tatkawng**), Terminalia maryocarpa (**Char**), Amura wallichi (Thehleikhak), Michelia champaca (**Ngiau hnah hlai**), Callophyum inophyllum (**Sentezel**), Mesua fercea (**Herhse**) etc. On lower levels of slope bamboos of different kinds along with cane occur in abundance. Some other species like Dipterocarpus macrocarpus (**Thingsen**), Terminalia chebula (**Reraw**), Duabanga sonneratioides (**Zuang**) syzizumcumini (**Lenhmui**), Cinnamomumverum (**Thakthing**), Cinamomum tamala (**Tezpata**) etc. are also common in these forests.

(2) Tropical Semi Evergreen Forests:

These forests are generally limited to the north, north western and central parts of the state and cover larger area than any other types. Important species in these forests include Michilia champaca, Schima wallichi (**Khiang**), Gmelina arborea (**Thlanvawng**), Toona ciliate (**Teipui**), Chukrassia tabularis (**Zawngtei**), Sterculia villosa (**Khawpui**), Sterculia colarata (**Khaukhin**), Podocarpus nerifolia (**Tufar**), Adina cordofolia (**Lungkhup**), Bomax ceiba (**Phunchawng**), Dillenia indica (**Kawrthindeng**) etc. Bamboo and cane though occur in abundance, are generally found in the shady low-lying areas.

In relatively drier areas of wet evergreen and semi evergreen forests, however, deciduous trees predominate. They abound in species like Juglans regia (**Khawkherh**), Emblica offcinalis (**Sunhlu**), Macranga peltala (**Hnahkhar nu**), Castonopsis tribuloides (**Thingsia**), Sapium baccatum (**Thingvawkpui**), Gmelina arborea, Albizia procera (**Kangtek**), Albizia lebbeck (**Thingchawk**), Sterculia villosa etc.

(3) Montane Sub-Tropical Pine Forests:

These forests are generally found at higher altitude along the eastern bound ary of the state where the climate is relatively cooler with decreasing amount of rainfall. Common species in these forests are Pinus keseiya (**Far**), Quercus incana (**Phen**), Quercus serrata (**Sasawthing**), Schima wallichi, Prunus cerasoides (**Tlaizawng**), Myrica esculenta (**Keifang**), Rhododendron kingianum (**Chhawklei**), Eupatorium odorata (**Tlangsam**), Cleroendrum colebrookianum (**Phuihnam**).

Despite a very large area considered being under vegetal cover the forests in Mizoram are reported to be under stocked. On an average, the forests in the state are believed to have a growth of 35 cum (cubic meter) of stock per hectare against 74.42 cum/ hectare at national level (Patnaik, 2000:22). The stock growth at present level will not be able to meet the growing needs of the people. The demand for forest products especially timber and fuel wood

Names in parentheses are local representatives of species/ genera has been rising consequent upon population growth and changing life style in the state. Forest Survey of India in 1991 reported per capita annual consumption of fuel wood in the state to be about 1.6 cum. Timber consumption was reported to be around 0.2 cum per capita/annum. Fuel wood and timber consumption in the state is believed to be around 15,000,000 cum and 190,000 cum respectively in 2000-2001. It is projected to rise to 2,480,000 cum and 3,10,000 cum in the same order by 2015 (Patnaik, 2000:23). It is, thus, imperative that forests of Mizoram are not only conserved but also expanded to meet the growing needs of the people.

Deforestation and Emerging Issues

Forests, apart from their environmental significance, have always been serving as an important resource base to meet the economic needs of the people especially for those who maintained a symbiotic relationship with them. But the growth of industrialization and need to develop infrastructure have led to commercial exploitation of forests even in remotest areas.

The first major exploitation of forests in India was started by the British administrators in the wake of development of rail transport after 1853. The demand for over "one million railway sleepers translated into an unregulated assault on forests". Realization that the "forests were not inexhaustible" led the British government to form Imperial Forest Department in 1864 to ensure uninterrupted supply and sustained yields from forests. But the conventional definition of forests enshrined in the Indian Forest Act of 1865, as "land covered with trees, brush wood and jungle, restricted the government to raise plantations on barren lands. The government, therefore, vested the power of use of forests in itself through the promulgation of the Forest Act, 1878. The British government despite oppositions established its right over forest resources at the cost of customary rights of the people. It shied away from defining forest but "classified them into three categories on the basis of functions assigned to them – (i) Reserved Forests; (ii) protected Forests; and (iii) Village Forests. The classification still persists. Reserved forests were meant for commercial exploitation and people were debarred from exercising their customary rights to use resources of such forests. Protected forests though were supposed to record the rights of the people, it could never be settled. It forbade "grazing of animals or any use perceived as harmful to the forests. Such forests could also be converted to 'Reserved forest' when necessity was felt (Rastogi; 2007:40). The Forest Act, 1927 reinforced the earlier Act. Same mind set appears to be continuing in India even after its independence. The National Forest Policy, 1952, categorized forests as (a) Protection Forests; (b) National Forests; (c) Village Forests;

and (d) Private Forests and tree lands wherein the functions of Protection and Village forests remained unchanged. But National Forests were marked to meet 'defense, communication and industry needs with an emphasis on increasing their yields. Private forest owners were given full rights over their forests but communities were allowed only 'limited rights' in the form of servitude and only in certain classes of forests. Appropriation of the rights of the communities between 1947 and 1971 was aimed at revenue generation for the state against "fulfilling local needs" (Rastogi, 2007:42). The problem further aggravated when National Commission on Agriculture (NCA) also in charge of forests in 1976 considered tribal rights and privileges to have brought destruction to the forests. It considered "production of industrial woods to be the raison d'etre for the existence of forests" (Rastogi, 2007:42). The impression that the states were diverting forest lands for non-forest purposes led to the shift of forest from State List to Concurrent List through the Forest Conservation Act (FCA), 1980. Seizure of settlement powers from the states made millions of tribal and forest dwellers unauthorized occupants of the forest and use of forest resources by them as illegal since 25th October 1980. It also envisaged stopping jhum or shifting cultivation in forests under government control –forests, definition of which has ever been changing. Shift in perception and attitude towards forest have led to many controversies and legal battles mostly in connection with ownership and settlement of lands to real owners within notified forest areas despite acknowledgment in the National Forest Policy document, 1988 that "a symbiotic relationship existed between tribal and forests, and that people living in and around forests depended on it for their livelihood and survival". A December 2006 verdict of the Supreme Court of India acknowledged the fact and passed an order to restore the land rights to the people in forest areas. In the same vein, the Apex Court also defined the forest and accepted the dictionary meaning of forest as "a large tract of land covered with trees and undergrowth sometimes mixed with pastures; the trees growing in such a tract".

However, different agencies have attempted to define forests in accordance with their purpose. Thus, United Nations Convention on Combating Desertification defines forests as a "dense canopy with multi-layered structure including large trees in the upper storey". Food and Agricultural Organization of the U.N.O. considers an area over 0.5 hectares of trees with no other predominant land uses to be a forest. United Nations Framework Convention on Climatic Change defines forests as areas that have "young natural stands and all plantations which have yet to reach a crown density of 10-30 per cent or tree height of 2-5 meters including the areas which may be temporarily unstocked".

But in present economic-political situation the Government of India through its Ministry of Environment and Forest (MoEF) is all set to redefine forest in the light of its:

(1) International commitments and different orders of the apex court of the country; and

(2) Ecology concerns and social desirability.

A definition of forest by the Ashoka Trust for Research in Ecology and the Environment (ATREE), a consultant of the MoEF, is accordingly proposed as "an area under Government control, notified or recorded as forest under any Act, for conservation and management of ecological and biological resources" (Guha, 2001). It, thus, proposes to assign all the rights to the Government. If community forests are considered beyond the purview of the definition (which they will not be) then, it may concretize the apprehension that the land under them will be made available for sale to any body willing to pay through governmental arbitration for, ownership of such forests will be impossible to establish. There will be every possibility that such forest areas are put to non- forest use. It must have been this fear that prompted the Apex Court of the country in 1996 to ban felling of trees in forests to counter "government – timber lobby nexus especially in India's north east". It was then estimated that the region was loosing more than 31,700 hectares of forest every year.

In case of Mizoram, where 33 per cent, out of 87 per cent forest area, is owned by communities (Poffenberger et. al., 2006: 9) land can easily be transferred with stands of trees which may adversely affect the communities economically and go against the requirement of territorial environment conservation. The power of notification and its withdrawal vested in government (MoEF) and its attempt to encourage partnership with private entrepreneurs through the Department of Land Revenue may also be viewed as an attempt to transfer forest lands to them in the name of afforestation and social forestry as well as stakes in ever expanding global economy.

References

Anon, (1994) : Soil Erosion and Land Degradation Problem in Mizoram Institute of Resource Development and Social Management (IRDAS); Hyderabad.

Bali, J.S. (1988) : Report -Soil Conservation Society of India, New-Delhi

Burchfiel, B.Clark : Physical Geology: Structure and Processes of the Earth; Charles & Merrill. Pub. Co, Sydney

Gautam, NC. (1995) : "Concept and Delineation of Watershe for Development"; Annals; NAGI:XV(1)

Glendinning, Robert M. (1959) : 'Land as Resource' in Natural Resources; (eds) Martin, R. Huberty and Logan Richard, F.; Warren, L. Flock; McGraw Hill Book Co. Inc: New York.

Gunju, J.L. (1975) : "Geology of Mizoram"; Bull. Geol. Min. Met. Soc. India ;48 :17-26.

Guha, R. (2001) : The Pre History of Community, Forestry in Environmental History (Quoted by A. Rastogi (2007) Down to Earth, June 15, p: 42).

Haggett, P. (1983) : Geography: A Modern Synthesis; Harper & Row New York.

Huntington, E. (1951) : Principles of Human Geography; Joh Wiley & Sons, New-York.

Kellman, Martin (1975) : Plant Geography, Metheun & Co. Ltd. London.

Klages, K.H.W. (1958) : Ecological Crop Geography: MacMillan, New York.

Krishnan, M.S. and (1940): "Did the Indo Brahma River Exist ? Rec. Ayenger, N.K GSI IXXV, Paper 6

Masson, H.L. (1957) : "Language Analysis and the Concept and Langenhein, J.H. Environment" Ecology 38.

Nandi, D. (1983) : "Tectonic Evolution of Tripura Mizoram Fold Belt, Surma. Basin, North Eastern India"; Quar. Jour. Geol. Min. Met. Soc. India 55 (4) :186-194.

Pascoe, E.H. (1919) : "The Indobrahm"; Quart. Journal Geological Soc; IXXV.

Patnaik, S.S. (2000) : Status of Forests and Prospects of Agro forestry in Mizoram'; in Souvenir, International Workshop on Agro forestry and Forest Products; NEHU (Mizoram Campus, Aizawl) 28-30 Nov., 2000.

Patterson, S.S (1956) : The forest Area of the World and Its Potential Productivity; Geography Deptt.; Royal University of Gotenberg; Sweden.

Pilgrim, G.E. (1919) : "The Siwali River"; Journ. Asiatic Society, Bengal, XV(New Series).

Piffenberger, M. (2006) : 'Forest Sector Review of North East India' in Community Forestry International; Down to Earth' 15th June.

Rastogi, A. (2007) : Down to Earth; 15th June.

Raunkiar, C. (1934) : The life Form of Plant; (Transl.) H. Gilbert Carter, Oxford, London.

Singh, J. (2003) : India: A Comprehensive Systematic Geography; Gyanodaya Prakashan; Gorakhpur.

Singh, Jasbir (1971) : Agricultural geography of Haryana, Kurukshetra.

Singh, R.L. (1971) : Cited in India. A Comprehensive Systematic Geography. J. Singh; op.cit.

Thomas, M.F. (1969) : "Geogmorphology and Land Classification in Tropical Africa" in Environment and Landuse in Africa (eds) M.F.Thomas and G.F. Whillington; Methun & Co.; London.

Thornbury, W.D. (2002) : Principles of Geomorphology; (Indian Reprint) New Age International Publishers; New Delhi.

Tiwari R.P.; Lalnuntluanga; Kachhara, R.P. and Singh, B (1996) : "Landslide hazard Zonation Mapping, Hrangchalkawn, Mizoram: Journ. Engg. Geol.XXV(1-4)

Tiwari R.P.; Barman, G. and Satsangi, P.P. (1997) : "Miocene Crabs from Mizoram, India", Journ. Paleonto logical Society of India; 42 pp. 127 -132.

Tiwari R.P.; Mishra, V.P. and Lyngdoh, B.C. (1998) : "Lower Miocene Fish Teeth from Mizoram, India, Geo Science. Journal, XIX(1)

Wadia, D.N. (1975) : Geology of India, 4th ed. Tata McGraw Hill; New Delhi

Warming, E. (1909) : Oecology of Plants; (Trans) P.Groom and L.B. Belfour: Oxford, London

PART II

THE PEOPLE

2

The People

Mizoram a tiny state in the womb of remote hills is generally believed to be devoid of much of natural resources. Arguably the state has a very vast forest resource (over 79% of the area under forest cover with certain varieties of commercial and exotic species). It, however, possesses one of the greatest resources - its people. With a distinct culture Mizos are open to learn and adapt to the ways and means of the fast changing world. With .08% (2001) of national population the state ranks 28th amongst the States and Union Territories. The rate of population growth in the state has been recorded at 2.88% per annum against 2.12% at all India level which itself is considered very high in comparison to world average of about 1.6%.

Not only resource utilization but also its creation and processing, however, must be considered in context of population (Zimmerman 1951) only. The state of Mizoram despite the paucity of natural resources, in conventional sense, is believed to be far from having negative man-resource equilibrium. In fact, with 42 persons / km^2 (2001), the state may generally be considered under populated. However, at the present rate of growth the state may soon join the category of overpopulated areas for, the carrying capacity of the hill terrains is generally considered to be low. Even presently, the pressure on the quantum of 'known resources' appears to be immense as the people of Mizoram appear to have graduated suddenly from a primitive subsistence economy to advance consumer stage without going much through the consolidation of intermediary phases of economy. This is generally reflected in the population dynamics within the state where rural-urban dichotomy is distinctive and is getting aggravated. Quality and standard of living are being compromised despite the fact that per capita income (Rs. 21,327/-) and performance in social sector in Mizoram is much better than most of the states in the country. In fact, Mizoram ranks 6th on development index for the country (India Today, September, 24, 2007). But performance on economic front and the state's capacity to regenerate, and expand economy and sustain the process of development is suspect (Ray, 2005). Almost half of the total population has concentrated in 22 urban centers of the state which have grown without much operation of dynamic urban processes. They appear nothing more than crowded dens of humanity around certain administrative centers. About 37% of the people in the state live below poverty line. In a supposedly closely knit society like that of the Mizos, this is the greatest challenge that the people and the administration have to confront. In order to bring about equitable distribution of developmental benefits the state needs to harness the quality of its population for its own sake.

The present chapter is an attempt to analyze the population characteristics of Mizoram. Growth and distribution pattern of population impinge on behavior of movement with special emphasis on social bearings (Bhattacharya, 1978, i). It also influences the economy, polity, ecology/environment and the society (Chaubey, 2000). It will be the quality of its human resource that will decide the future of economic growth and process of development in the state in days to come.

Growth of Population

Despite the fact that India adopted census operations since 1750, population figures for the state of Mizoram prior to 1971 may not be very reliable. This may be attributed mainly to the remoteness and inaccessibility of the area till late sixties. Secondly, the significance of the area dawned only by the latter part of the 19th century on British rulers when the Lushei Hills was brought directly under the colonial administration. Christian Missionaries also made incursions in the area almost simultaneously. Moreover due to fluid political boundary with Burma which was administratively separated from India in 1937 and also in the wake of formation of East Pakistan in 1947 the census operations and their reliability in these parts of the country have remained suspect. However, after the Independence of India and since first census operations under free India in 1951 the population statistics may be considered fairly accurate though many areas within the political boundary of the present state could be enumerated for the first time only in 1961 and 1971. In terms of absolute number it may not have much significance but it would certainly reflect substantially in percentile change in a small population.

Census of India recorded the population figures for the state of Mizoram at 82,432 persons in 1901 which has since grown to 888573 in 2001 – a progressive growth of about 245% in last 100 years at an exponential rate of growth of 37.5%. Decadal growth of population in Mizoram has been given in the following table 2.1.

Population growth in Mizoram before 1971 has been inconsistent (Fig. 14). The reason for inconsistency before and after Independence of India may however, be attributed to different factors in those seven decades. First decade 1901-11 experienced the consolidation of British military encampments and the then civil administration. This was also a time when Christian Missionaries started making headway in Mizoram through their charitable establishments helping in deceleration of inter tribal wars. The state experienced slowing down of

TABLE: 2-1
Growth of population in Mizoram with decadal variations since 1901.

Year	*Population*	*Decadal*	*Growth Rate (Decadal)*	*Decadal Exponantial Growth Rate (in %)*	*Annual Exponantial Growth Rate (in %)*
1901	82434				
1911	91204	8770	10.64	37	
1921	98406	7202	7.90	37	(-) 0.09
1931	124404	25998	26.42	38	0.59
1941	152786	28382	22.81	38	(-) 0.11
1951	196202	43416	28.42	38	0.17
1961	266063	69861	35.61	38	0.21
1971	332390	66327	24.93	38	(-) 0.31
1981	493757	161367	48.55	38	0.66
1991	689756	195999	39.69	38	(-) 0.24
2001*	888573	198817	28.8	38	(-) 0.3

Based on Census of India 1981, Series 31, Mizoram, Part - II-A, General Population Tables, p-26.

• *Census of India, 2001*

population growth during 1911-21. This coincided with the negative growth rate at national level. It may be explained by the withdrawal of troops from Mizo soils in the wake of 1st World War and concomitant impact on civil administration and the activities of the Missionaries. 1931 again saw the reinforcement of army camps and civil administration along with expansion of Missionaries' activities. Slowing of peopling has again been recorded in 1941 which again may be attributed to the on set of 2nd World War in which quite a number of locals also took part away from their home land. Population growth during this period may also have been affected by the inter-tribal feuds albeit lesser in frequency and magnitude, as well as dwindling skirmishes with British administration that took substantial toll of at least male lives.1951 on wards, there has been progressively substantial growth in the number of people in the state consequent upon many factors operating together (Fig.13). Inter tribal feuds were gradually ceding and local administration was reorganized. It was during this period that the Lushai Hills attained the district status under the state of Assam. There had also been relative control over the rate of infant mortality and fatal diseases. At the same time new enumeration units were also incorporated for census purposes.

The rate of growth in 1961, thus, was recorded to be over 35% despite the fact that a natural calamity in the form of famine caused by Mautam* visited Mizoram in late 1950s. The real impact of it, however, could be realized only in 1971 census. Compounded with the insurgency of the late sixties, the 1971 census recorded sagging in growth rate. It may be attributed to loss of lives and difficulties in the head count of underground outfits It could only partially be compensated by the induction of military and paramilitary forces and strengthening of civil administration. Also some more areas were enumerated for the first time in 1971. And though a positive growth of 24.93% was recorded it was about 11% below the previous decade. 1971

**Mautam refers to famine consequent upon bamboo flowering. Bamboo flowering is believed to have a larger cycle of 50 years and shortest cycle of 25 years.*

for many reasons may be considered a 'demographic divide' in the peopling history of Mizoram. Since then the population has continuously been rising. The peak growth rate was recorded in 1981 when the state experienced an increase of more than 48% over previous decade. Such a high rate of increase may be attributed to proportionately large scale immigration necessitated by the requirements of administrative set up of a newly formed Union Territory of Mizoram in 1972. Development schemes and counter insurgency measures to bring the people of the area in the national main streams required the service of different sections of people in the reconstruction and development of the state. So a large number of workers, teachers, and administrators from different parts of the country joined the local population.

The process of integration with the Indian Union culminated in the recognition of Mizoram as full fledged state on 20th February, 1987. Subsequent censuses recorded gradual slowing in the rate of population increase. Apparently population in Mizoram appears to be moving towards stabilization though growth rate is still very high. However, it is of significance that the real population figures fell below the projected increase estimated in 1996 (Singh, 1998) by about 11% from an estimated increase of 39.96% to only 28.8% in 2001.

In general, five phases of population growth may be recognized in Mizoram (i) a static phase till 1921, (ii) high increase till 1961 with intervening decrease in the wake of 2nd World War (iii) declining phase ending in 1971 (iv) Phase of highest growth next decade and (v) Declining trend of growth since. Declining trend in growth rate of population, however, is a function of many factors which simultaneously operate in the state. It must be realized that though the death rate has been contained substantially, the birth control measures, despite growing awareness, has yet to gain acceptability by the larger section of the Mizo society. Therefore, the decline in the rate of population growth is hard to be attributed to the decline in natural growth rate. This, on the other hand, may be attributed

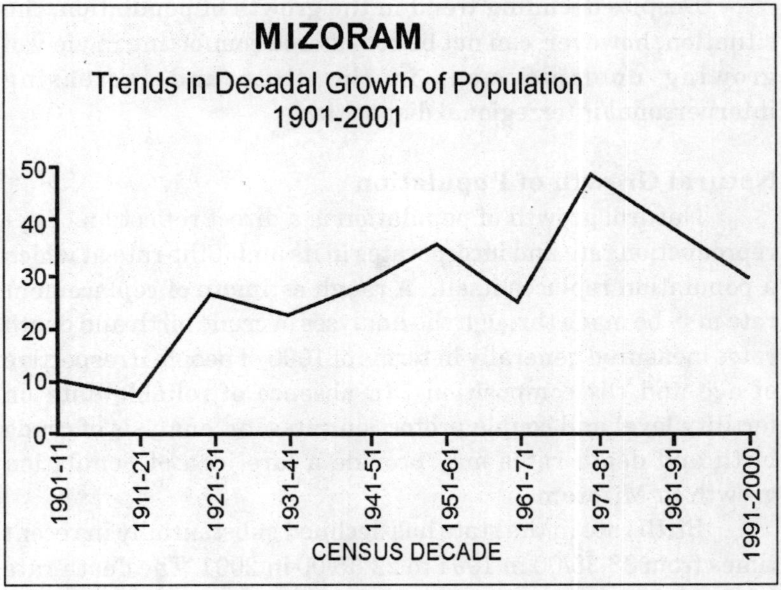

Fig. 13

to two major factors: Firstly, with high literacy rate a very substantial number of people migrate to other parts of the country in pursuance of higher studies. Also, people are found responsive to job opportunities even beyond the state boundaries which had been an anathema to them till recently. However, magnitude of worker emigration is negligible. Secondly, with the statehood in 1987, the ethnic upsurgence and an attempt towards ethnic cleansing by certain section of the society is taking its toll and reflects in declining trend of the population growth. Moreover, growing demand of populace on local job market for the works earlier carried out by the migrant workers as well as increasingly successful entrepreneurship of the Mizos to expand in different sectors of economy are leaving little opportunities for immigrant population. And though some illegal migration from across the international borders may still be persisting it must be of lower magnitude as compared to the total immigration experienced between 1971 and 1981.

Despite declining trend in the growth of population, the situation, however, can not be considered comforting in view of growing unemployment in the state and increasing interpersonal/interregional disparities.

Natural Growth of Population

Natural growth of population is a direct reflection of net reproduction rate and incorporates in its ambit the rate at which a population replaces itself. A rough estimate of replacement rate may be made through the analyses of crude birth and death rates measured generally in terms of 1000 of people irrespective of age and sex composition. In absence of reliable data on fertility level and couple protection rates, an analysis of crude birth and death rates may provide a fare idea of population growth in Mizoram.

Birth rate in the state has declined substantially in recent times from 38.35/00 in 1991 to 22.35/00 in 2001. The death rate in the same period declined from 7.94/00 to 5.29/00. A mid decadal estimate for birth and death rates at 30.6/00 and 6.6/00 per annum respectively would suggest a natural growth of population at the rate of 24/00. Such a growth rate would add about 165500 persons to the population of 1991 against the actual addition of 198817 persons in 2001. This would amount to an additional increase to the magnitude of about 33300 or 4.8%. The rate of population growth recorded between 1991 and 2001 corresponds with the figure that takes into account natural growth and migrant population (24% natural growth + 4.8% migrant population = 28.8%) With the present trend of the rate of population growth the population of Mizoram is expected to attain stability by 2041.

This is interesting to note that a section of scholars do not give much credence to the idea of population control. For them the relationship between population growth and economic development need not necessarily be negative particularly in view of advancing technology and changing economic patterns. It may even help in growth of economy thereby generating funds for investment in social sector.

For some scholars like Kausik Basu (2002) issue of population growth particularly with reference to the third world countries are highlighted disproportionately to perpetuate hegemony of Developed Economies. Yet there is no denying the fact that unbridled growth of population as contemporary experiences suggest, leads to degeneration of grave magnitude in the polity and economic structures of the society. It raises questions about socio cultural, economic and physical security – (Siddartha; 1991:1-59). Even greater is the question of sustainability of environment. The existing circumstances in the state of Mizoram show a great imbalance between the number of people and the economic infrastructure as well as the level and rate of economic growth. It also raises questions about the state's capacity to sustain its economy even at a modest level of living standard.

Sub-regional Growth of Population

Population growth in Mizoram, however, has not been uniform. There have been significant variations in sub regional and micro level trends since 1971. The following table 2:2 gives trend of decadal growth at block level.

It is obvious from the table and fig.14 that population growth at micro level has been much influenced by the changing administrative significance of the districts and blocks since 1981. In the wake of the formation of the new state people gravitated towards centers of administration and political power. Thus, out of the 22 R.D. Blocks in the state only six registered growth above the state average. Highest number of people was attracted towards the state capital Aizawl housed in Tlangnuam Block. Thus, it recorded highest growth of more than 78% over 1981 population. The southern blocks of Chawngte and Lawngtlai due to their autonomous District Council Status and their location along the Bangladesh border registered a very high growth that may partly be attributed to migration from across the border in post Indo-Pak War of 1971. Lunglei, the second biggest urban center after Aizawl and itself

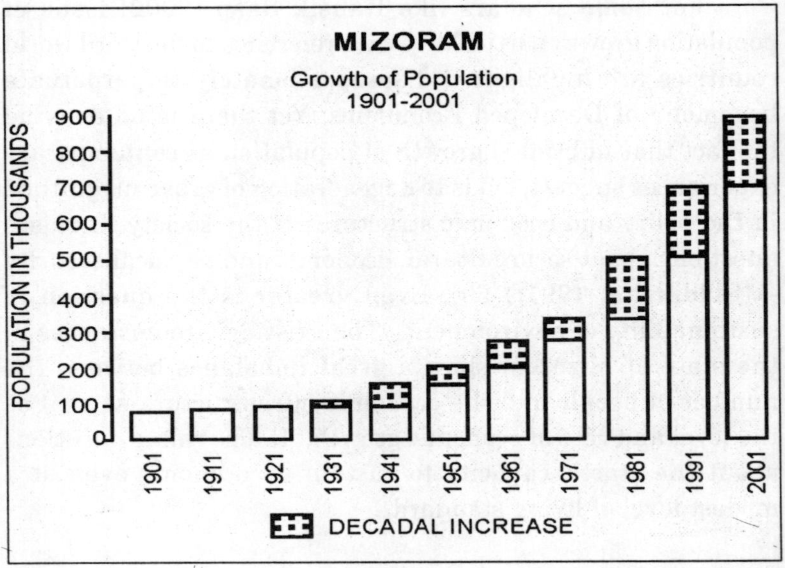

Fig. 14

an important center for district administration appears to have attracted people from its vicinity. In Saiha district, the population gathered near the district headquarters of Saiha in Tuipang Block leaving the block of Sangau with a modest growth of about 22.5%. Such selective concentration of population is also obvious from the fact that 6 of the blocks during the period registered negative growth (Table-2:2).

During the period 1991-2001, however, 11 blocks registered a growth rate above the state average of 28.8% (Fig 15). It may be attributed to the formation of new districts and addition of two blocks in 1998. Thus, Thingdawl which registered a negative growth during 1981-91 periods registered a growth of over 32% in 2001 with the formation of Kolasib District. Incidentally Thingdawl is the only R.D. Block under the administration of Kolasib district (a new R.D. Block Bilkhawtlir was carved out of the existing area of Thingdawl Block in 2004). Similarly, E.Lungdar under the newly formed district of Serchhip gained more importance as block headquarters hence positive growth in 2001 though nominal,. On the other hand, Serchhip

TABLE: 2:2

Table showing growth of population in Mizoram at Block level since 1981.

Growth of Population at Block Level*

Sl. No.	Name of the Block	Population in 1981	1981-91	1991-2001
			Growth (in %)	
1.	Aibawk	11671	23.73	14.39
2.	Darlawn	20870	0.54	17.22
3.	Phullen	11993	(-) 13.22	27.92
4.	Thingsulthliah	24107	12.39	21.21
5.	Tlangnuam	95835	78.08	27.99
6.	Ngopa	8963	44.37	34.05
7.	Khawbung	14320	(-) 3.73	39.16
8.	Khawzawl	28320	77.23	32.67
9.	Reiek	12467	(-) 2.72	14.83
10.	W. Phaileng	16838	28.23	(-) 4.06
11.	Zawlnuam	28761	7.27	(-) 9.89

(Contd.)

(Contd. Table 2:2)

Sl. No.	*Name of the Block*	*Population in 1981*	*Growth (in %)* 1981-91	*Growth (in %)* 1991-2001
12.	E. Lungdar	18892	(-) 1.78	1.92
13.	Serchhip	26554	12.59	30.12
14.	Thingdawl	45020	(-) 0.42	32.12
15.	Bunghmun	12239	27.04	6.17
16.	Hnahthial	22781	(-) 8.36	15.66
17.	Lunglei	34530	40.49	33.76
18.	Lungsen	23300	13.72	15.88
19.	Chawngte	16983	45.44	34.33
20.	Lawngtlai	18517	58.39	31.55
21.	Sangau	8777	22.43	35.28
22.	Tuipang	22143	57.75	32.24
MIZORAM	493757	38.55	28.	

Figures for 1981 and 1991 are adjusted in accordance with the reorganization of Blocks in 1998. Till 1991, there were Three Districts and 20 R.D.Blocks.

Population Change 1991-2001
(District Wise)

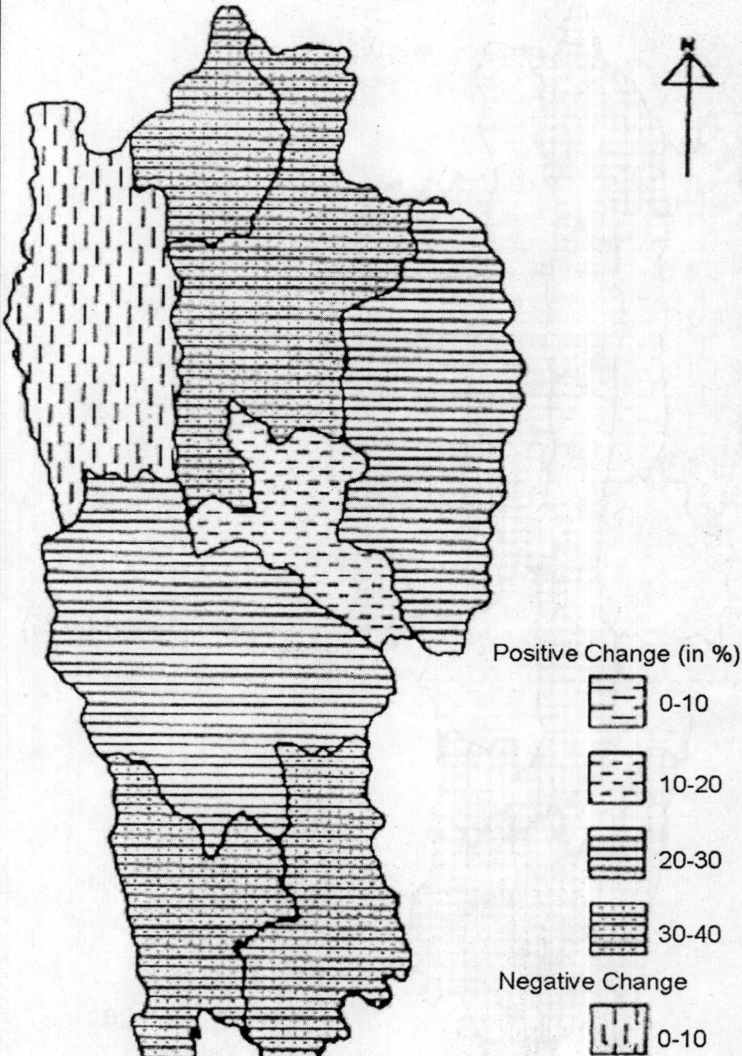

Fig. 15

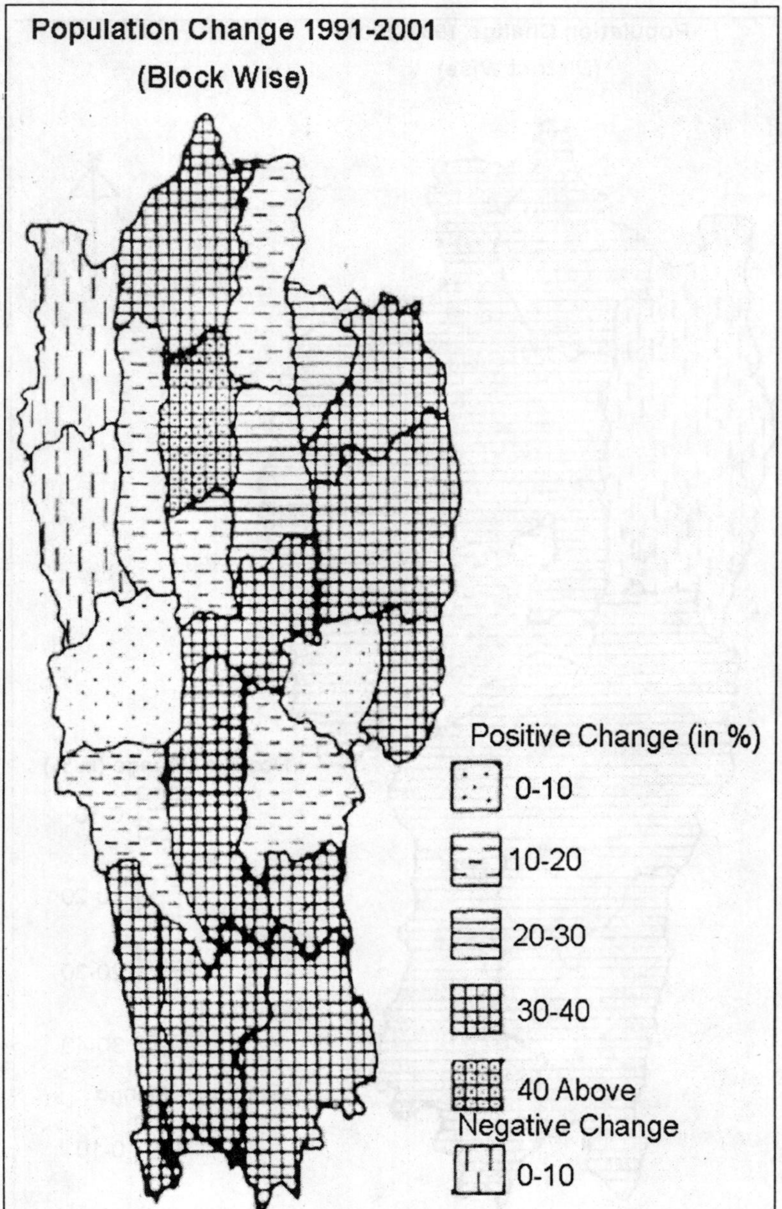
Population Change 1991-2001
(Block Wise)
Positive Change (in %)
0-10
10-20
20-30
30-40
40 Above
Negative Change
0-10
KILOMETRES
10 5 0 10 20 30 40

Fig. 16

grew drastically and, it may safely be assumed at the cost of its peripheral settlements.

Notable is the fact that the two blocks of W. Phaileng and Zawlnuam in Mamit district registered a negative growth in 2001 against modest to insignificant positive growth between 1981 and 1991. Such a trend in the district may be attributed to the volatile situation along the border with Tripura and caused by the tensions created by the Bru movement and Riang problem.

It, thus, appears that in absence of much economic bases it is the administrative significance of the places which has influenced the population growth at sub state level in Mizoram.

Distribution of Population

Distribution of population in Mizoram though apparently appears to have been influenced by topographical characteristics historical antecedence of settlements is no less significant. It had generally been the consideration of strategic advantages against feuding groups that led the Mizos to locate their settlements at ridge lines. Traditionally, thus, the distribution of settlements in the state following the alignment of hills has been linear in pattern (Fig. 18). Slopes and valleys by and large have remained unoccupied. This also is reflected in distribution of population density which is very uneven in Mizoram both at district as well as Block levels. It ranges from as low as 21 persons in the district of Mamit to a little over 91 persons per sq.km. in Aizawl District (Fig. 19). On an average, however, the density of population, according to 2001 census, was recorded to be 42/km^2 at state level- an increase of about 9 persons /km^2 against 32 persons in 1991.

Variations in the distribution of population becomes more apparent at Block levels where density of population is found to vary between as low as 12/km^2 in the Block of Bunghmun to as high as 474/km^2 in Tlangnuam.

It is obvious from the table2:3 that only two districts namely Aizawl and Kolasib have higher density of population than the state average. Aizawl district with strong urban base

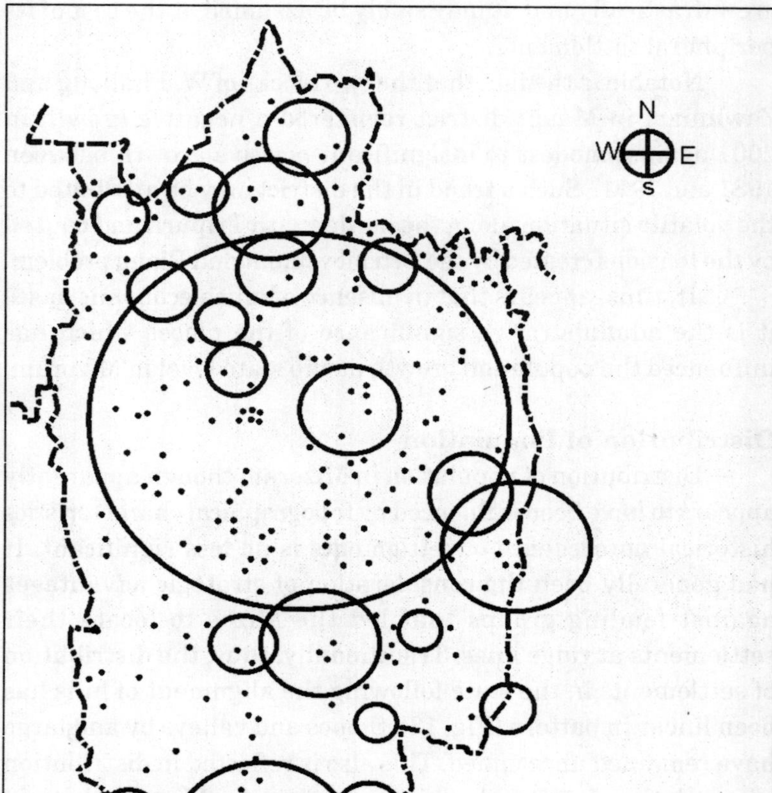

Fig. 17

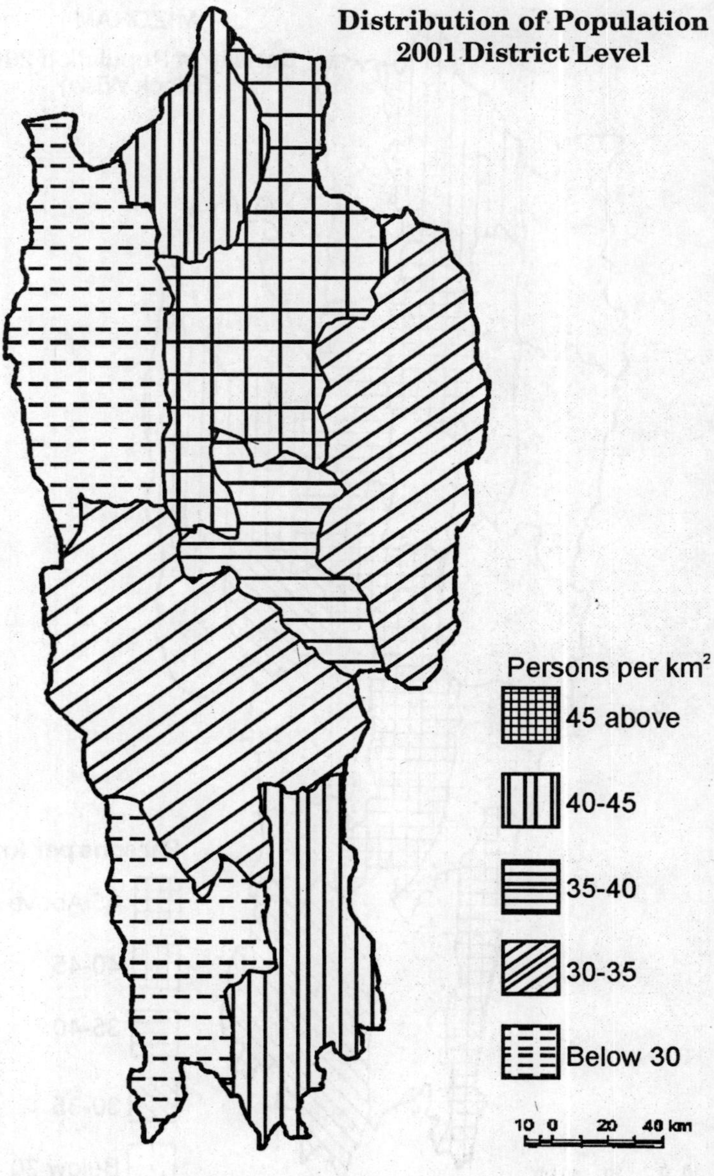

Source : Statistical Handbook 2002, Directorate of Economics & Statistics

Fig. 18

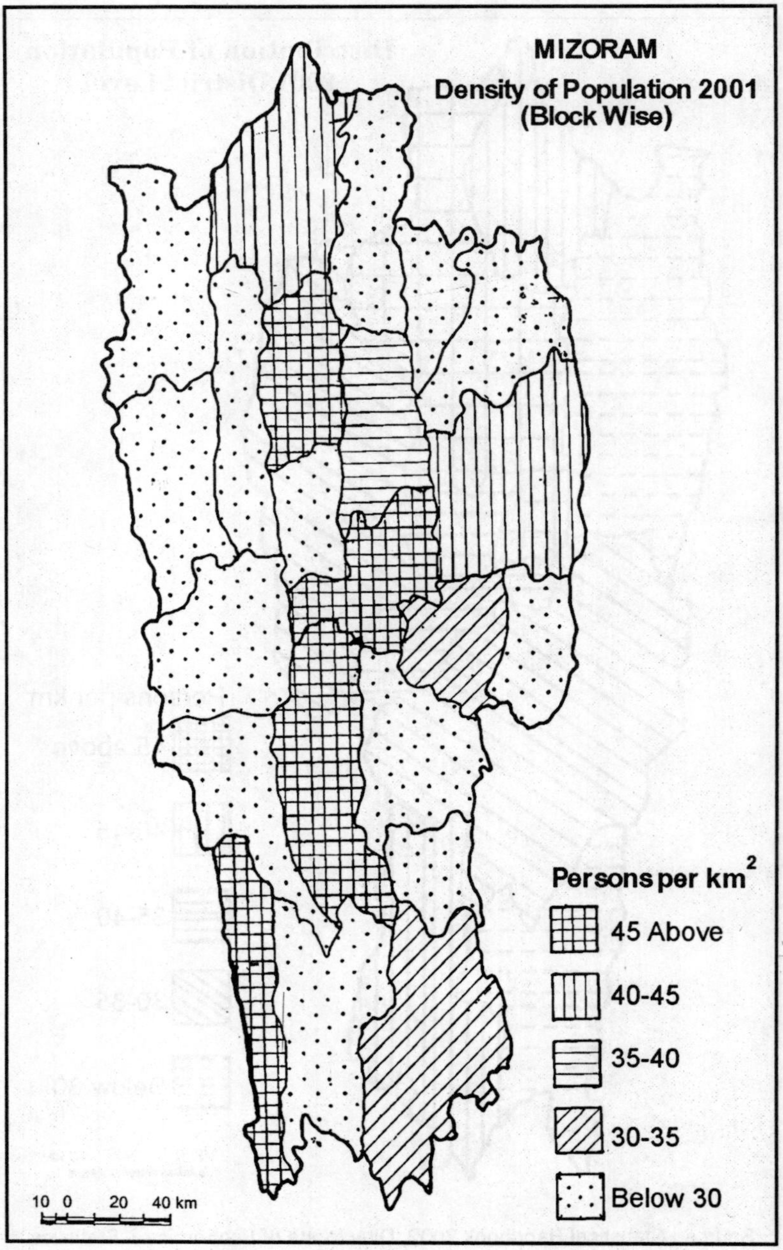
MIZORAM
Density of Population 2001
(Block Wise)
Persons per km^2
45 Above
40-45
35-40
30-35
Below 30
10 0 20 40 km

Fig. 19

accounts for more than 30 percent of the total population of the state in about 17% of the state's area. Similarly, the district of Kolasib with about 6.56% of the State's area supports over 4% of the population of the state. Closest to the density of 42/km^2 is the district of Serchhip with 41 persons per sq. km.

The district accounts for about 7% of the state area with a little less than 3% of the total population. It is noteworthy that these three districts together have 11 urban centers against 22 in the state and account for over 40% of the State's population. The density of population in the districts of Lawngtlai, Champhai, Saiha and Lunglei ranges between 36 to 30 / km^2 with 12%, 15%, 6.6% and 21.5% of the State's area respectively. The district of Mamit has the sparsest distribution of population. With over 14% of the total area, the district accounts for only 7% of the total population with a population density of only 21/km^2.

The hill states due to their limited carrying capacity and irregular terrain attributes for habitation generally have sparse population. Yet Mizoram shows a kind of variability which can not be considered normal. The northern districts of Kolasib, Mamit, Champhai, Aizawl and Serchhip contain about 70% of the people in the state. Even in these districts there are areal variations e.g. all blocks in Mamit district have less than half of the State's average density. This, however, may be attributed to the socio- political turmoil in the area and consequent negative growth of population in Zawlnuam and West Phaileng blocks. The people in search of peace and security have taken shelter elsewhere. It is reflected in density distribution of population in neighboring blocks of Tlangnuam with disproportionate concentration of people (474/km^2) and relatively higher crowding in Lunglei R.D. block (50/km^2) in southern part of the state (Fig. 20).

It may also be noted that the distribution of population in the state is much influenced by the administrative and historical significance of the centers in different blocks. Thus, Tlangnuam which houses the state capital and which till late 1990s acted as the district hub of northern Mizoram has the highest density of population. Larger concentration of people in the block has given rise to the growth of agglomeration economies and diversification of activities in non-basic sectors attracting more and more people.

Similarly, Lunglei the most significant administrative center of South Lushai Hills during British regime has retained its importance being located at the cross road joining southern districts of Saiha and Lawngtlai with the northern part and rest of the country. Squeezed between international boundaries with Bangladesh in the west and with Myanmar in south and east the people have also to depend on the market provided by Lunglei. Growth of market has set in diversification of non-

TABLE: 2:3

The following table shows the distribution of population at district and block level in Mizoram in 2001.

Sl. No.	*Name of Blocks / Districts*	*Density*
1.	Aibawk	27
2.	Darlawn	24
3.	Phullen	26
4.	Thingsulthliah	38
5.	Tlangnuam	474
Aizawl District		91
6.	Ngopa	19
7.	Khawbung	27
8.	Khawzawl	42
Champhai District		34
9.	Reiek	15
10.	W. Phaileng	21
11.	Zawlnuam	26
Mamit District		21
12.	E. Lungdar	30
13.	Serchhip	49
Serchhip District		38
14.	Thingdawl	48
Kolasib District		48

(Contd.)

(Contd. Table 2.3)

Sl. No.	*Name of Blocks / Districts*	*Density*
15.	Bunghmun	12
16.	Hnahthial	25
17.	Lungsen	29
18.	Lunglei	58
Lunglei District		30
19.	Sangau	25
20.	Tuipang	34
Saiha District		31

basic activities in the block. It has facilitated concentration of relatively larger population in the block.

It is also obvious that the blocks with better connectivity with the plains of Assam and consequently with rest of the country have relatively denser population e.g. Serchhip, Thingsulthliah and Thingdawl. Such skewed distribution of population however, does not bid well for a large area of the state and its resources remain unutilized or underutilized. Greater concentration of people in specific area is naturally leading to exploitation of human resource.

It leads to the growth of interpersonal disparities and has been found to beget disharmony caused by untoward behavior and stratification in the society. Such concentration, in addition, tells upon the fragile hill environment causing degeneration of life sustaining natural systems and infrastructural facilities. On the other hand, less dense areas, find it difficult to get infrastructural facilities extended as they fail to form strong power groups.

Population Composition: Sex Composition

Sex ratio is one of the most important indexes of socio-economic conditions and is fundamental to geographic analysis to an area. (Trewartha, 1953). The population of the two sexes impinges on the dynamics of demography in a regional complex. It affects the population growth, marriage rates (thereby reproduction rates) and occupational structure (Shyrock;

1976:105). It also reflects on the economy and is a useful tool in regional analysis (Franklin; 1956:168-69). It helps in understanding employment and consumption patterns, social needs and behavior of communities. Analysis of sex composition, thus, provides an additional tool to the study of evolution and growth of regional landscape.

It is one of the mysteries of genetics that male conceptions are more than females and though male mortality rate is generally higher than female mortality rate at all ages (Franklin; 1956) most of the societies have larger proportion of male population due probably to structure and compatibility of chromosomes in male (X; XX; XX; Y) and female (XX). The ratio of male conceptions to female conceptions is estimated to vary between 125-135 males for every 1000 females on global level (Stern; 1968: 429). Some estimates put it as high as 175 per 000 female (Chandana; 2000: 273). However, the other determinant of sex ratio is pre natal ratio. It is a fact that more male die before birth than female. Yet larger number of male conceptions keeps sex ratio favorable to masculine gender. It is characterized by excess of male at the time of birth in almost all societies (Ghose; 1946:7). However, where pre natal losses are great the society is less masculine than the societies where pre natal losses are less (Thompson & Lewis; 1965:74).

The sex ratio is further imbalanced in most of the developing regions of the world due to multiple racial and social stigmas (Chandana; 2000:277). Moreover, females die in developing countries due to negligence in infancy, childhood and old age (Gosal; 1961:124). Negligence and paucity of health facilities also lead to larger maternal mortality and lower life expectancy for female in general. Some of the societies have also evolved practices which go against the weaker sex. Sex ratio in these parts, thus, is generally more unfavorable e.g. against a world average of 993 females per 1000 male there are only 960 females/1000 males in Asia, and 933/1000 males (2001) in India.

India, however, shows much regional and temporal variation in sex ratio. In Mizoram also the variations are apparent though the communities here by and large do not have much prejudice against female child either at pre or post natal stage. Therefore, sex ratio is more balanced in the state than many other states of India. The average sex ratio for Mizoram was recorded to be 935 females per thousand males in 2001. It also reflected an improvement over 1991 ratio of 924 yet it falls short of supposedly an ideal ratio of 950 and above even in Indian context (Singh; 2003:36). A significant deviation in Mizoram from national scene is that urban sex ratio in the state at 948 is much better than the national average of 880/1000.

Sub-regional Variation

Regional variation in sex ratio in the state is generally influenced by the magnitude of migration both internal and external. Therefore, the areas having either perceivably more potentials for employment opportunities or are affected by certain socio-political turmoil, accordingly have been affected with regard to their sex compositions.

Most of the Districts in the state reflect a peculiarity in the distribution of sex ratio. In contradiction to national trend the sex ratio in urban parts of the districts is more favorable with the exception of Tuipang Another fact that stands out in the analysis of sex composition in the state is that newly formed districts (reorganization,1998) of Mamit, Kolasib, Serchhip carved out of the areas from Aizawl District in 1991, have significantly better urban sex ratio (Table: 2:4).

Reorganization of districts might have also affected urban sex ratio positively in Aizawl District having the state capital and other urban centers. Such positive urban sex ratio may be attributed to the customary movement of the entire Mizo family in the wake of migration. The only notable exception is the newly formed district of Champhai where urban sex ratio is probably skewed due to male dominated international migration from Myanmar as well as induction of persons to monitor trade activities along the border.

At block levels the sex ratio has been much affected by the connectivity of the blocks with district headquarters and

TABLE: 2:4

The following table shows sex ratio at District and R.D. Block level in Mizoram (2001).

Blocks / Districts / State	*Total*	*Rural*	*Urban*
Mizoram	935	923	948
1. Zawlnuam	925	926	923
2. W. Phaileng	844	844	0
3. Reiek	922	912	968
Mamit	896	889	933
4. Thingdawl	908	893	921
Kolasib	908	893	921
5. Darlawn	954	957	921
6. Phullen	937	937	0
7. Aibawk	957	957	0
8. Tlangnuam	962	915	964
9. Thingsulthliah	876	862	901
Aizawl	952	922	961
10. Ngopa	948	948	0
11. Khawzawl	933	965	912
12. Khawbung	967	967	0
Champhai	944	963	915
13. Serchhip	978	955	991
14. E. Lungdar	988	1008	959
Serchhip	978	955	991
15. W. Bunghmun	864	864	0
16. Lungsen	924	933	856
17. Lunglei	920	890	932
18. Hnahthial	963	987	908
Lunglei	922	920	924
19. Chawngte	923	923	0
20. Lawngtlai	878	878	0
Lawngtlai	899	899	0
21. Sangau	968	968	0
22. Tuipang	950	960	937
Saiha	954	963	937
Mizoram	935	923	948

the state capital. More inaccessible blocks have very favorable sex ratio as in case of E. Lungdar (988/00) Khawbung (967/00) and Tuipang (950/00) Darlawn (954/00) Ngopa (948/00) and Phullen (937/00) much above the state average. Sex ratio in Mizoram is also a reflection of high female literacy which enable them to seek employment to augment financial resources of the family. It is obvious from the fact that the work participation rate of females in the state is more than 47% - one of the highest in the country. The male folks particularly of poor families in many cases remain in the villages to look after their farming and other unmovable properties. On the other hand, the female folks generally the young ones, may be engaged as house helps by relatives in urban areasor attending schools there. Thus, the Blocks of West Phaileng (844/00) West Bunghmun (864/00), Thingsulthliah (876/00) and Lawngtlai (878/00) have a very disproportionate sex ratio. This also reinforces the view that unlike other parts of the country at least internal migration in the state is not male selective. And though the status of women in Mizoram is considered below par by many economically they appear to be better off when compared to conditions of the female folk in most part of the country.

Age Composition

Age composition is indicative of socio-economic history and development of a region. It is determined by three basic but interdependent variables of natality, mortality and mobility. Change in any one of the variables brings about change in other two variables and influence age-structure of a region (Clark, 1972:66). Areas with high fertility and low life expectancy rate as in developing regions have a very large young population in contrast to the developed regions which have low fertility and high life expectancy. The trend of age composition reflects on the existing and prospective population and the economy to certain extent. Similarly, migration influences population structure mostly in lower and middle age groups, for, mobility is generally induced in young generation for various socio-

TABLE: 2:5

The following Table gives the age and sex structure in Mizoram at state level in 2001.

Age Group	*Male (in %)*	*Female (in %)*
0-9	11.74	11.34
10-19	11.84	11.50
20-29	10.09	9.38
30-39	7.12	6.27
40-49	4.95	4.42
50-59	3.09	2.66
60-69	1.67	1.58
70-79	0.85	0.82
80 and above	0.68	0.36
	52.03	48.33

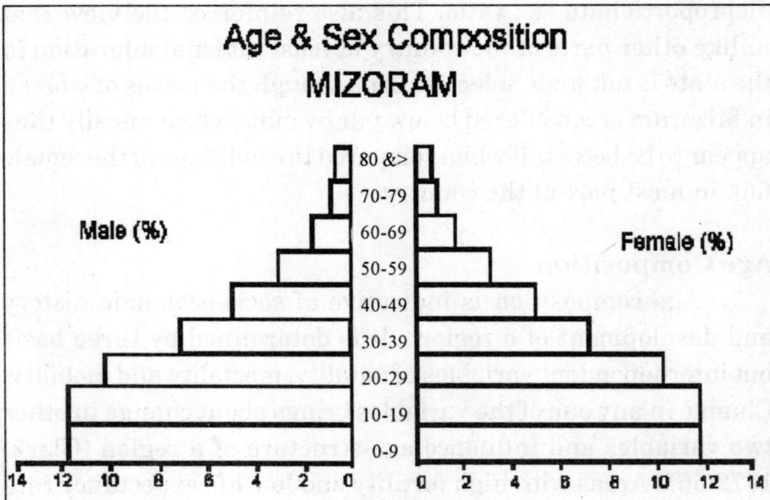

Fig. 20

economic reasons. Apart from the above mentioned, age composition may also be affected by socio-political tensions and strife that some times engulf a region. Age structure well represented by construction of age and sex pyramid for Mizoram may, thus, indicate the level of demographic transition in the

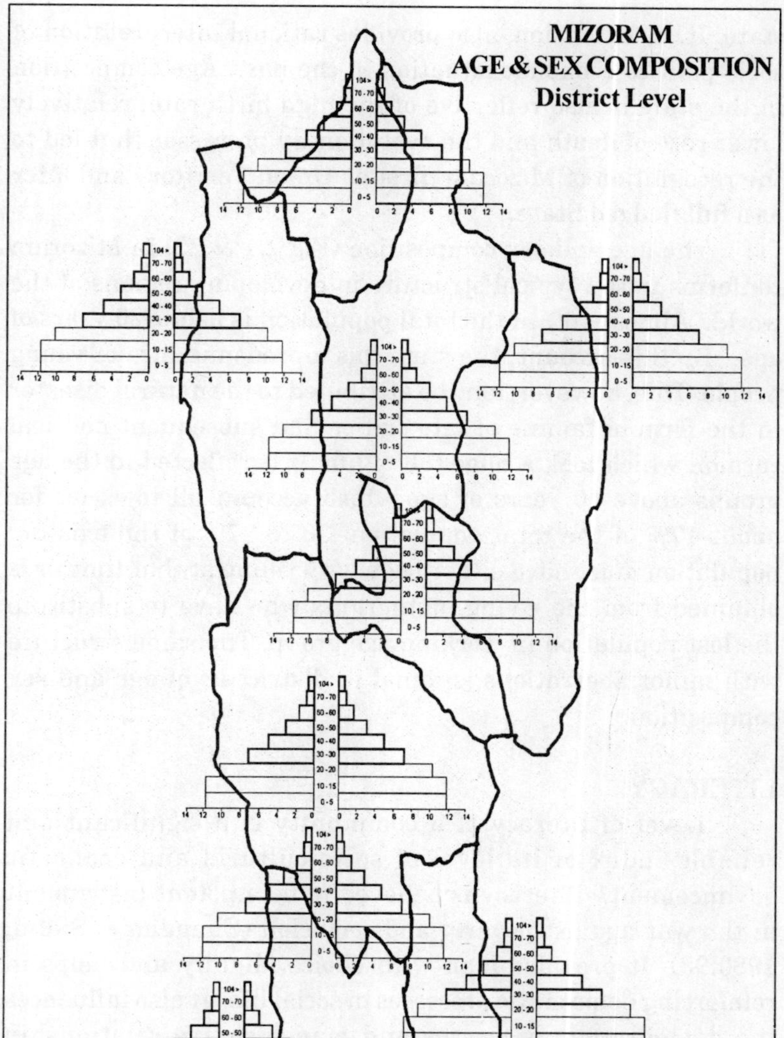

Fig. 21

state. It, by extension, also provides rational interpretation of socio-politico-economic situation in the past. Age composition in the state is also reflective of the high birth rate, relatively lower rate of death and the evolutionary processes that led to the recognition of Mizoram first as Union Territory and later as a full fledged State.

The age and sex composition (Fig. 21 & 22) in Mizoram conforms to the typical structure in developing regions of the world. Almost 46% of the total population is below 20 years of age. By this account, the state has a predominance of young people. This, however, may be attributed to the natural disaster in the form of famine of late sixties and subsequent political turmoil which took a huge toll of life. It is reflected in the age groups above 40 years of age which account all together for about 17% of the total population .36 to 37% of the existing population must have either been very young at that time or is obtained from the young immigrants who have to substitute the lost population in working age group. The same structure with minor aberrations is found in district level age and sex composition.

LITERACY

Level of literacy of a community is a significant and reliable index of its level of socio-cultural and economic advancement. Literacy is believed to be a potent instrument in the war against poverty and seclusion (Chandna & Sidhu; 1980:98). It provides man with choice, dignity and helps in reinforcing demo cratic processes in social life. It also influences the demographic processes and man-resource relationship through attitudinal shifts and institutional changes. Literacy in India is generally defined as one's capacity to read and write in his or her own language at least for enumeration purposes. Trewartha (1969:131) has been critical of this approach. Literacy, in fact, should enable one to comprehend and develop logical faculty to at least a certain level. It is in this light that the Population Commission of United Nations defined literacy as the capacity to read and write simple messages with comprehension in one's own language.

TABLE : 2.6

Table Showing District and Block wise Distribution of Literate Persons and the Difference in Male – Female Literacy.

Sl. No.	*Name of Blocks/ Districts*	*Literacy*	*Difference of Female Literacy (figures in %)*
1.	Aibawk	96.75	1.7
2.	Darlawn	91.60	3.2
3.	Phullen	93.70	3.0
4.	Thingsulthliah	.94.50	0.2
5.	Tlangnuam	97.35	0.2
Aizawl District		**96.5**	**2.92**
6.	Ngopa	88.2	6.4
7.	Khawbung	89.7	7.2
8.	Khawzawl	91.7	2.6
Champhai District		**91.2**	**5.4**
9.	Reiek	93.65	2.7
10.	W. Phaileng	58.50	18.4
11.	Zawlnuam	86.35	4.9
Mamit District		**79.1**	**11.11**
12.	E. Lungdar	94.0	0.6
13.	Serchhip	95.55	2.7
Serchhip District		**95.1**	**1.88**
14.	Thingdawl	91.3	6.6
Kolasib District		**91.3**	**6.6**
15.	Bunghmun	66.5	15.7
16.	Hnahthial	92.9	0.4
17.	Lungsen	57.35	22.5
18.	Lunglei	96.4	0.8
Lunglei District		**84.2**	**8.46**
19.	Chawngte	59.85	14.3
20.	Lawngtlai	68.20	11.8
Lawngtlai District		**64.7**	**13.82**
21.	Sangau	79.70	6
22.	Tuipang	82.85	8.7
Saiha District		**81.27**	**7.3**

Adopted from Age Data, Census of India, Mizoram (2001)

Most of the countries, therefore, define literacy accordingly. Literacy however alone can not be considered to indicate the quality of human resource in a region. It is the access to the quality of literacy which determines the capability of the people to take advantage of the resources and economic opportunities available in a region. By the present definition Mizoram has belied the demographers' understanding of spread of literacy. The present system of education was introduced in Mizoram by the Christian Missionaries and British administration in the first quarter of the 20th century. Though a late starter, the state with over 88% (2001) of its people classified as literates ranks 2nd amongst the States and Union Territories of the Indian Union. Education administration's earlier success in persuading the people to adopt a uniform language and script may be considered to be a single major factor behind this success. It got a boost when local soldiers actively participated in World War II and were exposed to the benefits of modern system of education. The significance of literacy further dawned upon the local populace during the insurgency periods of sixties and seventies.

It had been a time when passing of messages from one group to the other group(s) became a question of life and death. It required involvement of the local inhabitants who could understand the gravity of the messages and pass them undetected. Local language written in adopted Roman script with ingenious delivery system of a closely knit society reinforced the cause of the group which initially threatened cessation from the Indian Union. Involvement of the people was possible only if they attained at least a minimum level of capacity to read and write. Thus a population which had hardly 35% literates in 1951 recorded an impressive literacy rate of over 52% in 1971 – a period marred with political tension in the area. Once realizing the significance of education, Mizos have been fast to adapt to changing circumstances and widening economic opportunities in post insurgency period. Thus, 1981 and 1991 census respectively recorded 59.9% and over 81% of population as literate. The growth rate of literacy in the state surpassed many advanced states of India during this period. It left behind the Union Territory of Chandigarh and Delhi and became the second most literate state after Kerala in 1991. The trend continued when over 88% of its inhabitants were classified as literates in 2001.

Literacy level in the state on an average is much better than the national figure of just a little over 65%. There, however, exists substantial variation inregional distribution of literacy. Also, there is glaring disparity between the male-female ratios of literates in some parts of the state.

Again, the distribution of literacy is a reflection of the administrative significance of the districts and the blocks vis-à-vis the state. There are four districts which recorded over 85% literacy led by the district of Aizawl (96.5%) and followed by Serchhip (95.1%), Kolasib (91.3%) and Champhai (91.3%). The three districts of Lunglei, Saiha and Mamit with over 84%, 82% and 79% respectively may claim to attain and even exceed the present state average of 88.5% soon. The most disconcerting situation appears to be that of Lawngtlai district. With about 8.3% of the states population (the third largest concentration of people after Aizawl and Lunglei districts, the literacy rate (64.7%) reflects on the socio-economic conditions prevailing in the district.

Such trends are visible on sub-district levels also. Thus, against district average of over 84% in Lunglei district, Lungsen recorded a literacy percentage of only 57.4%; against 79.1% for Mamit the block of West Phaileng had only 58.55% and Chawngte had only 59.9% of its people classified as literates in Lawngtlai district (64.7%).

There also exists glaring discrepancy between the literacy of males and females in many blocks. In Lungsen (Lunglei District); West Phaileng and Zawlnuam (Mamit District), Chawngte and Lawngtlai (Lawngtlai District) and even in Tuipang

(Saiha District), Khawbung and Ngopa (Champhai District) the difference between male and female literacy is quite discernible where it ranges between the highest of 22.5% in Lungsen to a low of 5% in Zawlnuam. Literacy rate in urban centers of the state is over 90% against 81% at national level. However, there exists though insignificant, exceptions e.g. the towns of Khawzawl (86.7%) and Tlabung (89.1%) have relatively lower literacy than the state average.

The impact of high literacy in the state, however, has yet to be realized. Apparently, literacy has not been found to be an instrument of diversification of economy. This is reflected in still a very high percentage of working population engaged in primary activities (above 60%) or government sectors as well as in rising percentage of marginalized workforce (Kumar, 2006). This is indicative of the quality of education in the state which so far appears to have been failing in capability generation. The proportion of educational institutions (Primary Schools 1305; Middle Schools 804; High Schools 363, Higher Secondary Schools 31; Colleges 30) to the user age group ranging between 6 years and 29 years is certainly very high. Roughly, there is one primary school for 80 children; one middle school of 135; one High and Higher Secondary Schools for every 250 and one College for a population of every 3123 persons in the user age group. In fact, enrolment wise 89 students on an average utilize services of primary schools; 70 of middle schools, 133 of High and Higher Secondary Schools and 163 only of the Colleges in the state. Out of this onlyabout 10 students per school for HSLC examination; and about 31 students per college for degree courses manage to complete their education successfully. This needs to be viewed against the fact that the state claims to have one of the best teacher-taught ratio. The ratio at primary level is found to be 1:20; at Middle School 1:18; at high school 1:13; at higher secondary 1:16 and atdegree course level about 1:7 (2002-03). The input output ratio, thus, reflects on the quality of education in the state and development of its basic resource – its young population.

Economic Composition

Economic composition of a population provides a fair idea about the economic, demographic and cultural attributes of an area – the aspects that form the basis of regional development. It is indicative of the availability of persons in working age group and actual man power available to different sectors of economy. Man power refers to the section of population that has the capability 'to produce goods and services' and has the 'propensity to participate in the economically gainful activities' (Chandna; 2000:314). Depending on the actual participation in production process and services the workforce may be categorized as main and marginal. In Indian context, the main workforce includes that section of population, irrespective of sex, which finds engagement in productive activities for at least 183 days of a year. On the other hand, marginal workforce includes that section of population who may be engaged in productive activities for less than 183 days (Census of India, 2001). It is the proportion of the active working population that influence many demographic characteristics of a region like dependency ratio, replacement ratio and growth rates for working age group (Shyrock;1976: 202).

Workforce and work participation rates of a region are determined by many demographic, social and economic factors. They include birth rate, age structure and life expectancy, family size and behavior of migration; rate of literacy, marriage ages and health condition of the people. In addition, it is the type of economy, level of income and availability of opportunities that may influence the work participation rate. Any adverse condition may not allow the people to find gainful and durable productive engagement. On the other hand, high level of income of a family may find the members seeking activities not necessarily economically productive, at least for certain period of time. High income for a family or a community may be obtained by improving efficiency ment to them. Bare subsistence level economy in male dominated societies does not allow them to participate in decision making processes. In fact, they are generally exploited. It is evident by the fact that they are paid lower wages, particularly in the primary and secondary sectors of economy in most part of the developing world including India.

Composition of Workforce

Composition of workers the world over is dominated by male component of the population – a legacy that has come down since time immemorial. It, however, varies from area to area depending on the nature and exigencies of economy; level of literacy and social awakening; age and sex composition; degree of exposure of the people and status of women in society. There are also intra regional variations as these components may vary from one part to the other. Besides, there are determinants that make workforce composition of an urban settlement different from the rural ones. Such disparities are, however, more obvious in developing regions where migration from rural to urban settlement is dominated by male component of the society.

In most of the countries the major workforce is derived from the age groups ranging between 15-59/64 (Chandna; 2000:320) though in many developing regions child labor forms a substantial proportion of the workforce. Fortunately, the problem of child labor is almost non existent in Mizoram. Workforce in the stae is mostly composed of the people ranging in age between 15 and 59 years.

The state may boast of high proportion of workforce available to it. It, however, appears to have been caused by a very low proportion of population at higher age group over 60 years (see age and sex composition). Over 52% of the total population at state level has been classified as workers by census operations in 2001. This is, by far, a very high proportion when compared to national average of a little over 42%. Similarly, the proportion of female workers has also been found to be very high in the state - 44% against the national average of 26%. Workforce composition in the state, however, has been changing over time and so its proportion in different economic

Table: 2:7
Composition of Workforce in Mizoram

Workforce / Sector	*1991*	*2001*
Total Workers	**48.9**	**52.57**
Main Workers	**42.1**	**40.79**
Marginal Workers	**6.8**	**11.78**
Primary Sector	65.8	59.76
Secondary Sector	7.1	11.00
Tertiary Sector	29.1	3.24

sectors. The following table shows changes in workforce composition and workers' participation in different sectors of economy after 1991- the first census after Mizoram attained full statehood.

There, however, exists substantial variations in the proportion of workers at district and block levels. Though still very high it varies from over 60% workers in Serchhip district to a low proportion of about 44% in Saiha. At block level the variation is further accentuated. It varies from 70.8% in East Lungdar to a low of 40.8% in Tuipang.

Similarly, the proportion of female workers to the total worker also varies from a high of about 57% in Lunglei District to a low of 42% in Aizawl District. At Block level the fluctuation is still greater with over 69% in E. Lungdar to a low of about 36% in Tuipang. The following table shows the distribution of workers at district and block level in Mizoram.

It is noteworthy that though the population of female workers on state and districts levels is lower with the exception of Lunglei District, it is significantly very high in 17 out of the 22 blocks in the state. Most of the blocks which are almost entirely rural have a very high percentage of female workers. It is suggestive of the fact that male workers generally move away in search of better opportunities to bigger Urban Center. It is reflected in lower work participation rate in most of the blocks having big towns. The only exception is found in entirely rural blocks of Chawngte and Lawngtlai. Relative isolation and

Table: 2:8
Workforce Composition in Mizoram at Sub-state Level

State / District / Blocks	*Total Workers in % to total population*	*Female workers (in % total workforce)*	*Marginal workers (in % to total workers)*
Mizoram	52.57	43.70	11.8
Mamit	56.01	44.82	12.3
Zawlnuam	55.	51.06	10.1
W. Phaileng	54.0	50.9	15.9
Reiek	61.2	59.3	11.4
Kolasib	53.84	42.94	12.2
Thingdawl	53.0	49.6	12.1
Aizawl	50.04	42.02	11.6
Darlawn	63.5	62.3	14.7
Phullen	60.7	57.6	8.0
Aibawk	69.2	68.1	19.5
Tlangnuam	45.1	36.9	10.6
Thingsulthliah	64.1	59.1	14.1
Chaphai	62.86	46.88	17.0
Ngopa	61.9	60.4	14.5
Kawzawl	62.1	59.2	17.5
Khawbung	63.5	62.5	15.9
Serchhip	60.38	47.41	8.0
Serchhip	55.8	53.3	11.8
E. Lungsen	70.8	69.4	19.8
Lunglei	52.32	56.98	8.0
W. Bunghmun	58.8	54.5	10.6
Lungsen	54.8	52.4	7.8
Lunglei	46.4	38.3	6.0
Hnahthial	61.0	58.3	11.8
Lawngtlai	45.8	39.2	7.7
Chawngte	46.08	43.4	14.1
Lawngthai	45.8	39.2	7.7
Saiha	44.19	44.70	10.2
Sangau	55.7	54.2	13.1
Tuipang	40.8	36.3	9.3

hostile terrain coupled with ethnic distinction probably hinders the movement of workers away from their homeland. Higher participation of woman in economic activities, however, is not suggestive of better opportunities or higher level of development as is made out in the developed countries. The female workers are still home bound drawing sustenance from primitive agricultural activities in rural Mizoram.

Incidence of Marginal workers is also relatively high in rural areas and smaller towns, which attained urban status recently and have not been able to expand activities. Marginality of workforce in the state is also related with the level of literacy (Kumar, 2006) particularly in rural areas of the state.

It is, however, essential to diversify the economy in the state, because large working population does not necessarily helps in increasing the productive efficiency. A time has also come that workers attempt to find engagement beyond the state boundary to augment the economic resources of the state.

Urbanization

Urbanization is a process which embraces in it the dynamic sub-processes that influence the economic, social and political behavior and structure of a community. And together they operate to create spatial pattern' (Carter, 1982) distinct from the original. It is generally associated with concentration of non-agricultural occupation at advantageous locations (Rao and Tiwari, 1986:193). It attracts agricultural communities towards it (Carter, 1982) due to reduction in the need of farm labor consequent upon improved agricultural technology (Haggett; 1983:334) and increasing population pressure. The Process sets in a 'cascading effect of one activity upon another (Haggett; 1975:326). It is reinforced by people's attempt to find greater security and better means of survival. The process, thus, assigns multifunctional character to a settlement in sharp contrast to functional character of a rural habitat. Operation of processes, thus, obtained attain complexity due to 'interaction, integration and interdependence of the socio-political and economic subsystems'. Urban agglomeration in this regard play a significant role in creation, growth and diffusion of innovations as well as creation of subsystems there of' (Kumar; 1998:42). Proportional to their linkages they induce changes in 'morphology of settlements, degree of socio-economic awakening and the level of interaction. It also impinges on the value system and the way of life of the people in changing spatial pattern of interaction (Davis; 1967: 59) accordingly. The impact withers away with increasing distance from the urban core. Process of urbanization, therefore, may be considered indicative of the level of the use of human resource and socio-economic conditions of an area.

The distinction between ruralism and urbanism, however, may not be as sharp as it is made out to be. Basically it is a mental construct (Trewartha; 1953). The view is further reinforced when rural and urban settlements are believed to form a 'Unified field of social and economic relationships (Smails; 1966:45). Yet this is the dynamic nature of urban component of the population that is reflected by the changes in occupational structure and state of economy (Singh; 2003:37).This necessitates definition of urban settlement. Different countries, however, have adopted different definitions. Census operations in India has adopted four criteria to distinguish an urban settlement from that of a rural : (i) a settlement should have a threshold population of 5000; (ii) 3/4 th of its working population should be engaged in non-agricultural activities; (iii) the density of population should be more than 400 persons km2 and (iv) it should have a local autonomous administrative and regulatory body (in India such functions are carried out by municipalities or corporations or cantonment Boards or notified area committees). By such definition (except Aizawl which may be having a centralized administration after election for Municipal Council on 3rd November, 2010) none of the settlements in Mizoram 'satisfy the demographic and economic criteria of a census town'. All of the settlements which have been considered as urban have attained the status for having been notified by the State Government. They are, therefore, only statutory towns (Census of India, 1991, 1). The number of such towns increased from 1 in 1951 to two in 1971, 6 in 1981 and 22 in 1991.

TABLE: 2:9

Growth of Urban Population in Mizoram

Census Year	*No. of Towns*	*Urban Populations*	*% to the Total Population*
1951	1	6,956	3.54
1961	1	14, 257	5.34
1971	2	37, 759	11.36
1981	6	1, 21, 814	24.67
1991	22	3,77, 946	46.20
2001	22	4,41,006	49.63

Presently almost half of the population of the state (49.63%) resides in its urban centers (2001). It makes the state 5th most urbanized state amongst the union territories and states of India preceded only by Delhi (93.01%), Chandigarh (89.78%), Pondicherry (66.57%) and Goa (49.77%).

The growth of urban population in the state is a typical representation of the process of urbanization in third world countries. 'The process of urbanization appears to move around singular functions of settlements. The size and number of urban centers have grown consequent upon the expansion of non-basic activities set in motion in and around the nuclei of administration which provide service as the base for high density crowding (Kumar; 1998:43). They generally have become centers of economic power without developing much of the basic activities and factors of agglomeration economy. It is reflected in the growth of urban population in the state (Table: 2:9).

Population in Mizoram, however, has not been consistent at different urban centers. It appears that administratively significant urban centers have been growing at much faster rate than the intermediate or small towns.Also in the first decade after urban status being accorded almost all the centers registered a very high rate of population growth with the

Table: 2:10

Growth of population at different Urban centers in Mizoram

Name of the town	*Growth rate in census 1971-1981*	*Decades 1981-1991*	*1991-2001*
Zawlnuam	-	92.59*	(-) 9.70
Mamit	-	40.55*	44.111
Langpui	-	21.02*	34.02
Aizawl	137.7	108.40	47.05
Sairang	-	70.96*	42.53
Kolasib	36.13*	62.79	40.99
Vairengte	-	77.94*	37.60
Kawnpui	-	16.96*	22.34
Bairabi	-	21.35*	36.47
Darlawn	-	28.71*	7.09
Sercchhip	52.62*	86.71*	24.90
Thenzawl	-	44.02*	22.32
Saitual	-	142.20*	128.36
Khawzawl	-	66.33*	54.19
Khawhai	-	5.33*	14.32
Champhai	-78.90*	177.94*	27.18
Biate	-	17.46*	(-) 4.22
N. Vanlaiphai	-	19.27*	16.80
Tlabung	-	56.88*	7.98
Lunglei	185.84	106.91	32.41
Hnahthial	-	33.17*	28.66
Saiha	339.17*	94.77	45.04
Mizoram	**222.61**	**160.26**	**38.70**

notable exceptions of Zawlnuam and Biate which registered negative growths. The reason behind such growth may be attributed to socio-political tensions in and around Zawlnuam. In case of Biate it may be assigned to the movement towards newly formed district of Serchhip. Even the population growth in tf peopleownships of Kawnpui, Darlawn, Thenzawl, Khawhai, N. Vanlaiphai and Tlabung appear to be affected by migration to

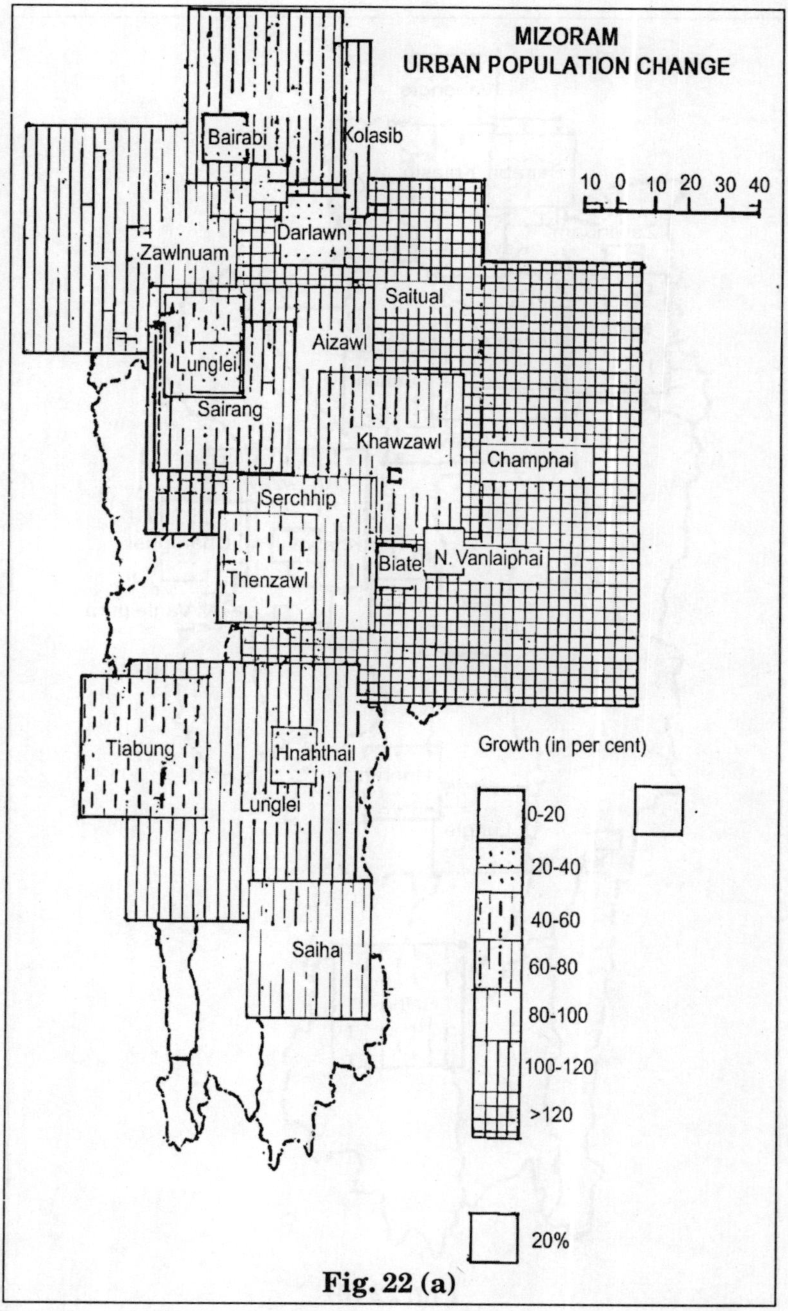
MIZORAM
URBAN POPULATION CHANGE
10 0 10 20 30 40
Bairabi
Kolasib
Darlawn
Zawlnuam
Saitual
Aizawl
Lunglei
Sairang
Khawzawl
Champhai
Serchhip
Thenzawl
Biate
N. Vanlaiphai
Tiabung
Hnahthail
Lunglei
Saiha
Growth (in per cent)
0-20
20-40
40-60
60-80
80-100
100-120
>120
20%

Fig. 22 (a)

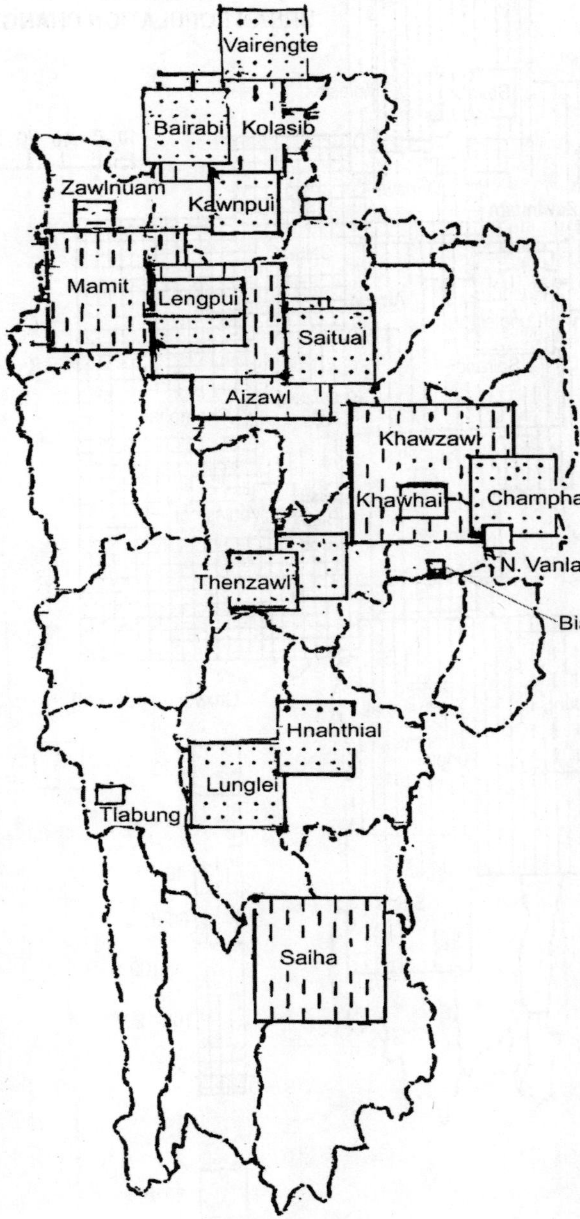
Vairengte
Bairabi
Kolasib
Zawlnuam
Kawnpui
Mamit
Lengpui
Saitual
Aizawl
Khawzawl
Khawhai
Champhai
N. Vanlaipura
Biate
Thenzawl
Hnahthial
Lunglei
Tlabung
Saiha

Fig. 22 (b)

bigger centers as their population growth hardly matches the natural growth rate of about 24% at state level. Table: 2:10 gives a comparative view of the growth of population at different urban centers since 1971.

It is obvious from the table that most of the settlements deemed to acquire urban status in 1981 registered phenomenal growth of population. In absence of true urban processes, however, they appear to be failing even in retaining their people. People, it appears tend to concentrate in larger urban centers like Aizawl, Lunglei, Kolasib, Champhai and Saiha

The rate of growth even in these centers has drastically dropped. It is suggestive of the fact that even big urban agglomerations in the state have not been able to generate economies which would sustain them in the long run. It is in this context only that McGee terms the process in third world countries as 'pseudo-urbanization' where in-migration from smaller towns to the bigger ones takes place as people find it difficult to go back to their roots in the villages (Hagendorn; 1987: 280).

SETTLEMENTS

Settlements refer to clustering of people at suitable locations and are associated with the 'establishment of permanent home'. The concept of 'settlement', thus, 'is inextricably related to the territory to which it belongs' (Singh; 2003:46). The settlements, therefore, are generally classified as rural and urban depending on the nature of derivation of sustenance. The cluster of people of rural settlements is generally referred to as villages where inhabitants are basically attached to agricultural activities and draw their sustenance primarily from the use of the surrounding uninhabited lands. On the contrary, the people of an urban settlement depend on non-agricultural activities and 'derive their livelihood from non-primary occupations'. Study of settlements focuses on the spatial and morphological characteristics of human occupancy of the area.

There are about 793 villages in Mizoram. But half of the state population lives in about 68 villages which now form the part of 22 notified towns in the state (towns in Mizoram are conglomeration of villages administered by independent village councils). Rests of the villages vary in sizes from a mere single house (census of India, 1991) in Leilet to over 1600 houses in Lawngtlai village (Block statistics, 2001). Many of the villages of certain tribes are shifted to facilitate Jhum cultivation particularly in southern part of the state. Identification of such villages is based on the local administration's acceptance (Census of India, 1991, 1). 54% of the total villages are located in the southern part of the state in the Districts of Lunglei, Saiha and Lawngtlai. But they account for only about 22% of the total population of the state. About 9% of the total population lives in the four towns of Lunglei, Hnahthial, Saiha and Tlabung. All together the southern part of the state accommodates about 31% of the total population with over 40% of the total area. The townships of the south also account for less than 18% of the total urban population in the state though it houses 2nd and 4th largest urban agglomerations. It is suggestive of the fact that there are large tracts of land which do not form a part of any settlement (Census of India – 1991,1). They, therefore, remain either unutilized or underutilized as state's resource.

On the other hand, northern part houses almost 46% of the total villages in 60% of the state's area. But they support less than 20% population. The northern part, however, supports 69% of the state's population. Almost 59% of its population is concentrated in 18 urban centers dotted all around the area. But Aizawl the capital agglomeration alone accommodates over 37% of the northern population. Other large urban centers with population over 10,000 together account for only 11% of the population in their half of the state. They include the townships of Champhai, Kolasib, Saitual and Khawzawl. Rest of the population is distributed in 13 other smaller townships. The density of population though is generally very low in all parts of Mizoram; in certain blocks of northern parts it is as high as 474 persons/km^2. Such a high rate of concentration in an area of fragile terrain may lead to irreparable damage to hill ecology.

Type of Rural Settlement

Rural settlements in Mizoram traditionally have been guided by what may be called 'optimization of man's protective space' (Singh; 2003:46). Most of the villages are located on ridge tops – a legacy obtained from the days of tribal wars. A strategic location has always been paramount in the minds of settlers. The settlement types for a brief period were disturbed due to grouping of villages during the period of insurgency between 1966 and 1986. Mizoram villages are generally located between elevations of 600 to 1500m and traditionally nucleated around the chieftain's residential quarters. The arrangement within the nucleus use to be based on social hierarchy within the village. In this respect these villages resembled the settlements in North Indian Plains. The type of rural settlement underwent a significant change after the abolition of chieftainship. Yet most of the clusters of houses maintain a kind of compactness. It probably has been necessitated by the historical experiences and need for co-operation in a hostile terrain. Most of the big villages have small hamlets, for contiguous areas for settlements are rare and far between. The hamlets may be separated either by steep slopes or water channels separating the inhabitable spurs.

The houses are generally compact with spacious but centrally located kitchen and one or two rooms with fragile partitions. The houses usually keep openings on valley side for wash disposal. Toilets are traditionally constructed a little away from the main house. The fronts built to level at higher elevations generally face the lane and pathways.

Pattern of Rural Settlement

As the settlements occupy the ridge tops they generally follow a linear pattern. Linearity of pattern has further been

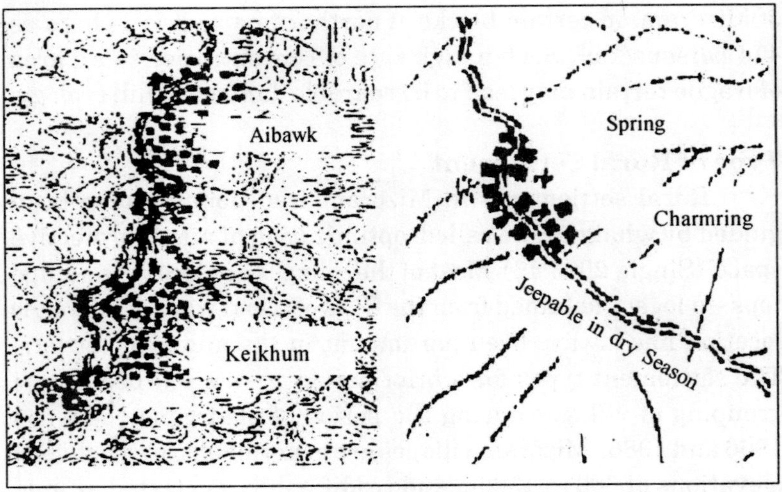

Plate 1(a)

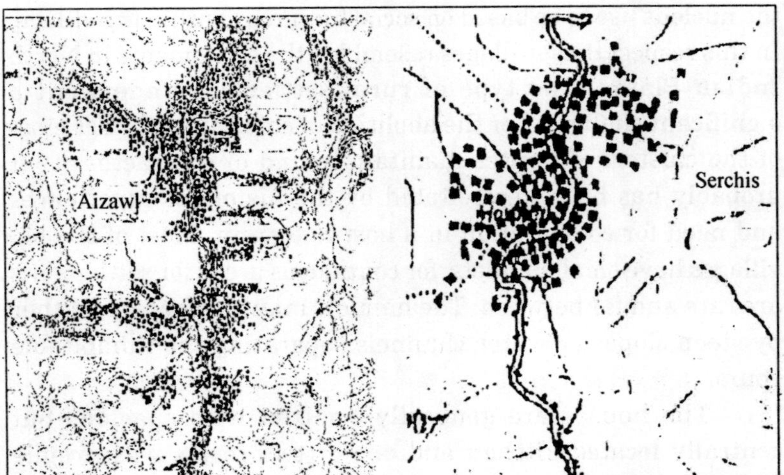

Plate 1(b)

augmented by transport lines monopolized by roads. Roads also for technical reasons generally follow the ridge lines. Only in large settlements where houses extend to occupy different spurs the linearity takes the form of star (plate:1)

The ground plans of these settlements have undergone substantial change in post chieftainship era. A further deviation was caused by grouping of villages for security reasons during insurgency period. Consequent upon large scale migration from rural settlements to urban centers and modification in functions of the settlements have influenced socially and culturally controlled social space in the villages. This is found to have affected the morphological attributes of the villages though the village units in Mizoram do not reflect segregations on the basis of caste based social structure as found in the villages particularly of North India. It may be of significance to note that most of the village in Mizoram is inhabited by members of the same clan. Thus, Social stratification does not have much meaning in the state. Growing Economic stratification, however, has a definite bearing on morphological attributes of the settlements.

Type of Urban Settlement

Urban growth in Mizoram is dominated by the primacy of settlements at Aizawl, the capital which following Jafferson (Singh; 2003:54) may be called a primate agglomeration. The town houses about 52% of the total urban population of the state. The second and third biggest agglomerations of Lunglei and Champhai house only about 11% and 6% of the urban population respectively. Thus, there does not appear to be much relationship between the distribution and sizes of the towns in the state. The phenomena may be explained on the basis of causes that have led to proliferation of townships.

It has not been generally the growth and diversification of functions which qualified most of the settlements as urban. It has only been the relative administrative significance that attracted and is still attracting the rural people towards it. Therefore, functions related with agglomeration economy are also proportional to the size of the urban settlements.

Therefore, most of the smaller towns still retain the morphological characteristics of a rural settlement albeit more compact. The functional classification of space is obvious in bigger centers only (Fig. 23).

Broadly, however, only three categories of functions may be recognized in these towns: (i) administrative, (ii) commercial,

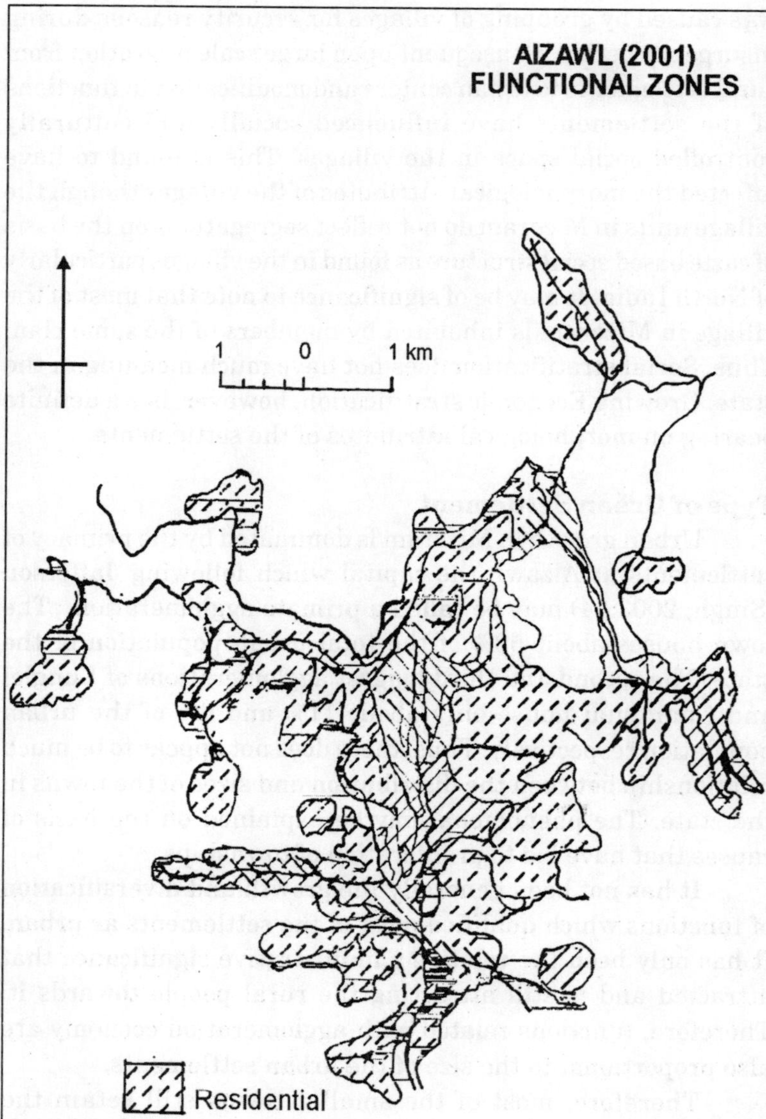
AIZAWL (2001)
FUNCTIONAL ZONES
1 0 1 km
Residential
Administrative & Institutional
Commercial

Fig. 23

and (iii) residential. Patterning of settlements in these towns is mostly controlled by the landform and the village councils of the area which are instrumental in issuance of lease for different purposes. Pressure of increasing population in these towns has forced growth of settlements on precarious slopes and adjoining spurs. It is not that only available infrastructural facilities of these towns have become vulnerable; it has been instrumental in bringing about shifts in land use pattern against all environmental constraints and principle of ecology.

References

Bhattacharya, A. (1978) : *Population Geography of India*, Shree Publishing House, New Delhi.

Carter, H. (1982) : The study of Urban Geography; Edward Arnold, Suffolk (UK).

Chandna, R.C. (2000) : *Geography of Population: Concepts, determinants and Patterns*, Kalyani Publishers, New Delhi.

Chandna , RC.& Siddhu, M.S. (1980) : *Introduction to Population Geography M / S Kalyana* Publishers, New Delhi.

Clark, John I (1972) : *Population Geography,* Pergamon Press, Oxford.

Chaubey, P.K. (2000) : 'India's Population Policy: Challenges Ahead and Strategies Therefor', Theme Paper I.I.P. A, New Delhi.

Davis, Kingley (1976) : 'The origin and growth of urbanization in the world' in Readings in Urban Geography, (eds) H.M. mayor and C.M. Cohn, University of Chicago; Chicago

Franklin, S.H. (1956) : 'The Pattern of Sex Ratio in New Zealand'; *Economic Geography* 32.

Ghose, D. (1946) : Pressure of Population and Economic Efficioency, Indian Council of World Affiars, New Delhi.

Gosal, G.S. (1961) : 'The Regionalism in Sex Composition of India Population', *Rural Sociology* 26.

Hagendorn, Jan S (1987) : *Economic Development*, Harper & Row; New York.

Haggett, P. (1975) : *Geography: A Modern Synthesis*, Harper International Edition, New York.

Ibid (1983) : Ibid, Harper & Row, New York.

Kumar, G. (1998) : 'Urbanization in Mizoram: The Emerging Trend' in *Urbanization in Mizoram: Retrospectand Prospects* (ed), Girindra Kumar Linkman Publication, Titagarh, West Bengal.

Kumar, G. (2006) : 'Literacy and Workforce structure of Rural and Urban Settlements in Aizawl District'; *Geographic,* Vol. 1.

Rao, VLS. Prakash (1986) : 'Urbanization in India: Spatial' in P.D. and Tiwari, VK. Mahadev (ed) Dimensions in Urban Geography, Heritage Oub. New Delhi.

Siddartha, K. (2000) : *Economic Geography: Theories, Process and Patterns*, Kisalaya Publication Pvt, Ltd, New Delhi.

Smailes, Arthur E. (1966) : *The Geography of Towns* : Hutchinson Univ. Library, London.

Singh, Jagdish (2003) : *India: A Comprehensive Systematic Geography*, Gyanodaya Prakasan, Gorakhpur.

Singh, R (1998) : "Population Statistics of Mizoram : A Study" in G. Kumar (ed) *Urbanization in Mizoram:Retrospect and Prospect*; op.cit.

Shyrock, H.S. (1976) : *The methods and materials of Demography*, Academic Press, New York.

Stern, Cutt (1968) : *Principles of Human Genetics.* Eurasia Publication House, New Delhi.

Thompson, W.S and Lewis, D.T. (1965) : *Population Problems*: Tata Mc Graw Hill, New Delhi

Trewartha, G.T. (1953) : 'A case for population Geography'; AAAG 43.

Ibid (1969) : *A Geography of population: World Patterns,* John Wiley & Sons New York.

Zimmerman, W (1951) : *World Resources and Industries*, Harper and Row, New York.

__________ (1991) : Census of India. Series 17, Part XII A&B, Mizoram.

__________ (2001) : Reports on Block Statistics; Directorate of Economics and Statistics, Government of Mizoram, Aizawl.

PART III

THE ECONOMY

3

The Economy

Economy and its changing nature play the most vital role in landscape evolution. Economic organization impinges on social and political structure and human behavior hence spatial organization of a region. It underscores 'spatial interaction' that involves specific spatial processes making areas 'discrete geographical entities'. Regional distributions are conceived as 'the product of processes and particularly of behavior' that is evidenced in 'decision made concerning human organization' (Ginsburg, 1968:11). Evolution of 'human organization' may be explained only in terms of orderly spatial processes of which economic processes are most significant. It must be noted that "ceaseless search for profitability within the interstices of world market has propelled a radical restructuring of national economies around the world" (Taylor et. al., 1995:3). The regional económies on sub-national level cannot remain untouched for, space-time compression consequent upon speed, innovation and progress induced by managers of resources in 2nd half of the 20th century has been on unprecedented scale (Harvey, 1990:418-34). It requires spatial restructuring which involves, in words of Schumpeter (1952:83) "creative destruction" of earlier system. In prevailing economic environment "the whole gamut of social activities is being turned upside down leaving no nook untouched" (Taylor et. al.1995: 4). Rural economies appear to be collapsing. Elites and proletariat alike, move towards cities – the perceived control centers. The rich migrate in order to stake their claims in the share of opportunities, the poor to cross the "poverty curtain". Economy in open global system is impinging on all aspects of man's social activities and necessitates redefinition of territorial relations on national and sub-national levels.

Economy of a region may, however, be judged in terms of utilization of manpower and exploitation of natural resources. They include in their ambit status of techniques and dynamism of socio-economic factors. It is the economic organization and function that separate developed areas from that of under developed – the two relative terms. The difference may be only in terms of actual use and potentiality for use. Thus, an under developed region may be identified with the one that "has good potential prospects for using more capital or more labor or more available natural resources, or all of these, to support its present population on a higher level of living (reflection of per capita income) or if its per capita income is already high to support a larger population on a not lower level of living (Viner, 1958:12).

This requires an understanding of under development. Under development of region, according to Jevons (1954:13) is characterized "by chronic mass poverty; and obsolete methods of production and Social organization". It means that "poverty", a synonym for low level of living," is not entirely due to poor natural resources and hence could be presumably lessened by methods already proved in other countries". Well-being of an economy, thus, requires to be assessed with regard to (a) per capita income; (b) occupational pattern; (c) population pressure; (d) employment generation capacity; (e) rate of capital formation; (f) distribution of wealth/assets; (g) quality of human capital; (h) level of technology; (i) level of living; and (j) demographic characteristics (Dutta and Sundharam,

(1981:4-9). With growing concern about environment degradation and re-look on induced change of consumer behavior, another aspect i.e. resilience of environment should also be taken as one of the parameter to evaluate the State of regional economy. At the same time, it must be realized that the above- mentioned parameters are reflections of interaction amongst political, economic and social situations that obtains in a region through adoption of the direction of national policies.

The state and people of Mizoram, though late starters are expected to adapt to demanding and changing economic environment in the country as well as contribute to the national economy. The change that has undertaken the state is by no means mean. A small state with 95% of tribal population appears to have attained certain spectacular growth particularly in social sector. It ranks 2nd in the list of literate states in India with 88.8% people being classified as literates. It is also the 2nd most urbanized state (5th including Union Territories) with 49.63% people inhabiting its 22 urban centers. It, in the country, commands the highest proportion of working population (52.7%) and highest per capita income amongst northeast Indian states. The state ranks 5th on Human Development Index amongst the states and Union Territories of India. All these achievements are without doubt commendable. Yet sustainability of these achievements and equitable distribution of the benefits of growth require to be addressed. Ray (2004) is of opinion that for an "economy like Mizoram in which a major percentage of income is exogenously sponsored by center, a special criterion needs to be followed to evaluate the performance of the state". Evaluation of the economic performance for the period 1993-94 to 1999-2000 suggests that NSDP at constant 1993-94 prices grew at a moderate rate of 4.8 per cent per annum against the national rate of 6.5 per cent. Per capita NSDP was registered as low as 2.25 per cent per annum against the national average of 4.56 per cent. NSDP grew at a rate of 5% per annum at constant price (1999-2000) during 10th plan period against 7.6 per cent at national level. Share of different sectors of economy to the State domestic product that may reflect structural transformation also does not show much change.

A look at the revenue sources of the state between 1992-93 and 2000-'01 suggests a very high dependence on devolution of resources from the central pool. It must, however, be noted that the central assistance has gradually been declining as necessitated by the course of economic reforms that government of India has been pursuing since 1991. During 1990-91, over 92 per cent of GSDP was contributed by the Centre in terms of grants etc. By 2000-01, the Central contribution though still very high as compared to an average 7 per cent assistance to other states came down to 66 per cent. Decrease in proportion of central assistance has been generally due to fall in the state share of central taxes. Mizoram was given a 23 per cent share during 1992-93, which came down to 5 per cent in 2000-01. Gross devolution of resources from the Centre, however, has been rising at a steady rate of 10 per cent per annum during the last decade of the 20th century. It is, but, a matter of concern that the trend might not continue for long owing to the necessity of structural adjustments in post Reform/Liberalization era. As a matter of fact, every state is expected to make accordant structural adjustments to face the challenges of new economic situations developing on global and national levels. At the same time they are expected to meet the aspirations of their subject.In this regard, it has to be cautiously noted that the growth of state Domestic Product in Mizoram is driven basically by service sector, which accounted for over 62 per cent of GSDP in 1999-2000. It was an improvement of 5 per cent over 1992-93. During 10th plan, tertiary sector contribution is estimated to be around 64.5 per cent. On the other hand, the share of primary sector came down from 33 per cent to 24 per cent during the same period. The same was estimated to have further dipped down to 20.5 per cent at the end of the 10th plan. Decline in the share of primary sector is accounted for by proportionate rise in contribution by secondary and tertiary sector. Such a change, in general perception, may give an idea that the structural change in the state is "moving towards a service sector one". But this requires serious examination particularly keeping in view production and productivity expenditures of the state. The following table gives the government's estimated liability with regard to revenue disbursement in 2005-06.

Table: 3:1

Revenue Disbursement Estimate in Mizoram (2005-06).

Sl.No.	*Major Heads*	*Rs. (In Crores)*	*Revenue (in %)*
1.	General Services	585.05	34.26
2.	Social Services	590.41	34.57
3.	Economic Services	532.17	31.16

Adopted from statistical Handbook; Mizoram: 2006; Directorate of Economics & Statistics; Govt. of Mizoram.

It is obvious from the table that not even 1/3rd of the revenue is made available to economic sectors which is basically concerned with enhancing production and its efficiency in the state. There too, the share of the cost of establishment (non-developmental expenditure) is high and recurring and needs serious consideration.

Ray (2004), in his study of financial sustainability of the state of Mizoram, thus, observes, "The poor performance of aggregate production and productivity reflects clear evidence of some lagging sectors and core sub-sectors". He further observes "the growth in agricultural income during 90s was registered even less than 2 per cent per annum with a growth of labor force of over 4 per cent. The overall income growth in primary sector that provides livelihood to 60 per cent of state work force (see table 2:7) had been less than even one per cent (0.54%). Moreover, high growth of landless agricultural laborer especially female laborer in a tribal state with favorable density (42 persons/ km^2) does not imply any improvement in purchasing capacity in agricultural sector. The relative share of secondary sector that hardly provides 6.5 per cent employment in the state, has improved by 3 per cent with a growth of about 7 per cent. However, the major component of secondary sector – manufacturing has registered a miserable negative growth of about (-) 13 per cent per year with its relative share of about 1 per cent in NSDP during 1999-2000. The growth and increase in relative share in the state income of secondary sector has been solely due to the unsustainable investments in construction by local elites who could not find any productive and employment generating alternatives for investment ......" "the tertiary sector has shown a clear sign of steady growth of over 6.5 per cent per annum during 90s with a contribution of about 63 per cent to state income in 1999-2000". Trend of performance (structural transformation) by different sectors of state economy may be visualized in fig 24.

Structural transformation in the state, however, does not appear to have strengthened its production base. Nor does it appear to have provided buoyancy to economy that could lead to diversification and capacity to generate productive employment. The primary sector still provides sustenance to about 60 per cent of the workforce. Proportion of marginal workers has been increasing alarmingly. From about 3.71 per cent in 1981 (pre statehood era) the number of marginal laborers rose to 7.07 per cent immediately after statehood in 1991. It further rose to 11.8 per cent in 2001. In addition, the problem of unemployment is becoming glaringly acute. It may be visualized from the fact that within one year between 2004-05 and 2005-06, according to the Employment Exchange of the state, unemployment grew by over 14.5 per cent. Actual figure may be much higher. It is also noteworthy that out of about 37200 persons on the live register of the Exchange 20500 persons are reported to have educational qualification above matriculation level. Substantial number of graduates (more than 4800), post

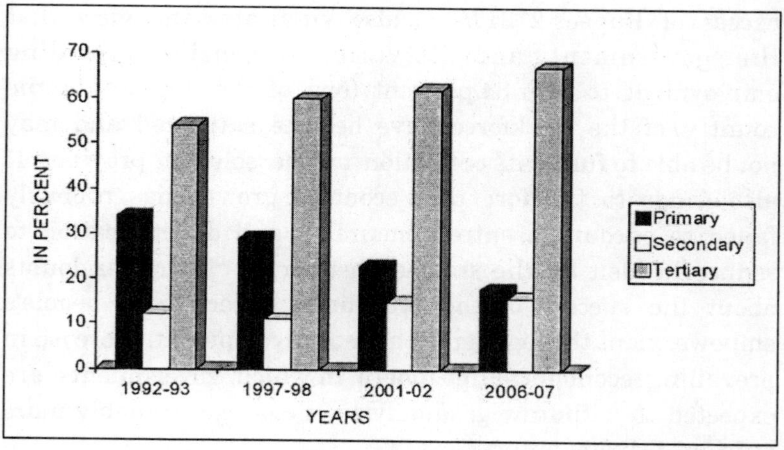

Fig. 24 (a)

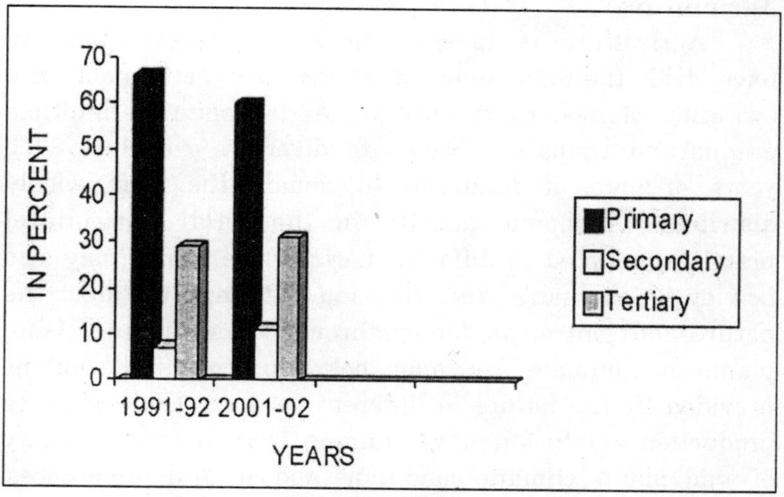

Fig. 24 (b)

graduate degree holders (about 1200) and persons with technical trainings in engineering courses and computer applications are reported to be unemployed. And though it is possible that many of them might be seeking placements at places of their liking it suggests lopsidedness of the economic growth and its centricity. It does not auger well for a state that claims to have a per capita income in excess of Rupees 21317/-. It also vindicates the view that the government and its various agencies providing employment to over 34 per cent (one of the highest in the country) of the workforce have become saturated and may not be able to fulfill its obligation as the sole job provider. It also brings to the fore that economic growth has probably failed to encourage entrepreneurship and diversification to reduce burden on the state exchequer. It also raises doubts about the success of the proclaimed objective of people's empowerment through growth and development. More so in prevailing economic atmosphere in which governments are expected to withdraw gradually to encourage, arguably more efficient private enterprises.

Agriculture

Agriculture as an economic activity is considered to have laid the foundation of community settlement and evolution of modern civilization. And despite its 'multiple origins' and changing thrusts to diversify over last 8000 years or more, it continues to remain the most widely distributed economic activity in the world. Agricultural practices, adopted in different parts of the world, may also be viewed as man's first conscious attempt to 'tame' the nature and control production through colonization of land, plants and animals. Yet, man took into account the options provided by the nature in different settings. Hence, diverse production and techniques obtaining from 'a unique legacy of wild plants, climatic conditions and cultural preferences' in which each region varies (Siddartha, 1999: 97). It is only after the technological revolution driven by the increasing use of inanimate energy sources in post 'Industrial Revolution' period that there has been an attempt to uniformize its operation and production, many times defying environmental constraints. It is reflected in dwindling number of cultivable species and changing productivity of land. Environmentalists are increasingly becoming concerned about lithosphere's and atmospheric changes causing disruption in spatial ecological balance and adverse effects on consumer's health. Modern agricultural techniques are believed, at least partially, to be responsible. They also believe that present practices are against the conventional wisdom of human communities, which gave due weight to interaction between the two sets of variables – physical and human.

In fact, most of the scholars who attempted to provide a scheme of agricultural typology and regionalization took this into account and concurred that 'ultimate limits of crop growth and livestock rearing was fixed by environmental conditions'. It implies the use of the land to be limited within the suitability and resilience of the natural conditions - the conditions, which guided the progress of human culture. Bennett (1944), thus, opined that "in recognition of the varying capacity of the land through the different geographic regions... 'Necessity of farming so as to maintain soil productivity, an adoptable system of agriculture has been devised to suit both the land and the farmer" (quoted by Whittlesay: 1936) to regionalize world agriculture in 5 major and 16 sub-groups which would also take into cognizance the cultural variants.

Agriculture in Mizoram

Agriculture in Mizoram traditionally has been subsistence oriented. Physical attributes of this hill state and transitory land occupancy in early days of settlements appear to have led to adoption of shifting cultivation (a primitive form of land utilization) in the Lushai Hills. The Mizo tribe as well as many other hill tribes of northeast India must have known it. It was and is still being practiced in many parts of Southeast Asian regions that these tribes traversed. Incidentally, shifting cultivation, known by various names in different parts of the world is probably the oldest form of agricultural practice. By its very nature, shifting cultivation (Jhum in North East India) is practiced by the farmer and his family on a 'self sufficiency basis' using simple implements. Thus, modification of landscape is minimal. It differs from 'agriculture' that is practiced with the greater use of tools and animals that brings about changes in landscape at faster rate. Thus, shifting cultivation has a singular merit that it is more environment friendly particularly in the tropical and subtropical areas. Other forms of agriculture that depend upon permanent clearings of land; use of different types of sophisticated deep tilling implements and fertilizers are suggested to be disrupting ecology. In addition, shifting cultivation is considered to promote community cohesion against modern agricultural practices that thrive on competition and individual handling of resources.

But shifting cultivation is suggested to be suffering from problems of under production, its inability to support ever-increasing population and changing capital intensive consumer behavior. These considerations make practice of shifting cultivation untenable. Yet, in Mizoram shifting cultivation seems to have been a way of life. And so change in cultivation practice has been slow despite many kinds of encouragement and assistance.

Mizoram is a state where agricultural operations are constrained by terrain attributes and primitive techniques. Historically, farming activities revolved round Jhum cycles and simple demands on land. Presently, however, due to reduction in jhum cycle consequent upon increasing population pressure and changing consumer behavior of the people the protagonists of development consider traditional farming practices as untenable. Thus, there have been attempts at substitution, not always in harmony with ecological characteristics of a fragile terrain dominated by hill and steep slopes. It is justified in order to enhance productivity through capital-intensive measures that generally go against small and marginal farmers (Hirway, 1984) who constitute the majority.

Despite all odds, agriculture continues to remain basic economic activity of the people of Mizoram. Though the contribution of agriculture together with allied activities (forestry, livestock rearing and fishing) has been falling in its share to GSDP (from almost 28.3% in 1996-97 to 22.04 % in 2001-02 to 20.03 in 2003-04), it still provides employment to over 60% of the total workforce (54.9% main workers + 5.7% marginal workers) in the state. During the same period number of agricultural holdings increased by 14.64 per cent from 65919 to 75576 ha. It is reported to have covered an area of 93198 hectares in 2003-04. Increase in number of holdings, however, does not necessarily suggest additional colonization of land for agricultural purposes. As a matter of fact, it appears to have been caused by fragmentation of agricultural holdings (Fig. 25.) in the state. 44.58% of the holdings belonged to the marginal farmers operating over land between 0.5 and 1.00 ha., 37.5 % to small farmers with 1.00 – 2.00 ha.; 16.58% to medium (4-10 ha) and 0.08% to large farmers having over 10 ha of land (Fig. 25)

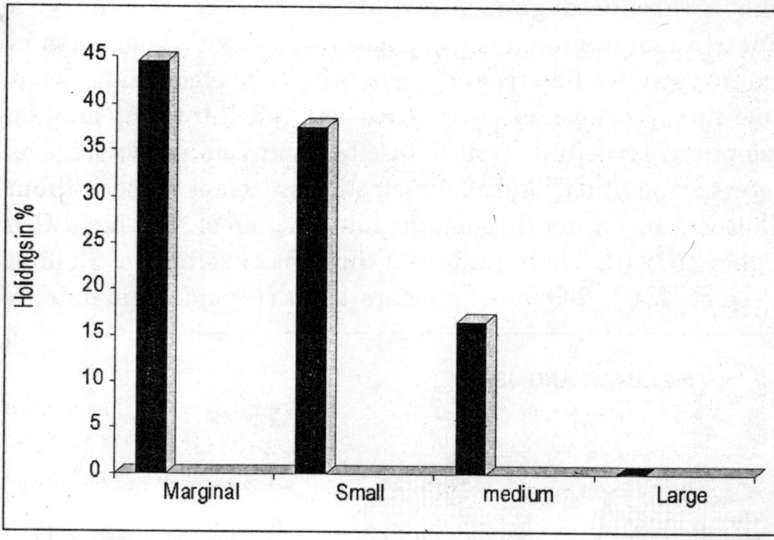

Fig. 25 Mizoram : Distribution of Agricultural Holdings

LAND USE PATTERN IN MIZORAM

Land use pattern in Mizoram, despite fluctuations in the size of land holdings, generally have been consistent (Fig. 26). But there are periodical variations in the intensity of land use.

Forests, so far, has been occupying the largest area followed by fallow lands (including current fallow), areas not available for cultivation (built up as well as barren and uncultivated waste), other uncultivated land (permanent pasture, grazing land under tree crops and cultivable waste) and net area sown. Table 3:2 gives an idea about the land use pattern in Mizoram over a period of six year taking into account penultimate years of 9th and 10th Plans i.e. 2000-01 and 2005-06.

Pattern of land use in Mizoram brings about certain disturbing facts as obvious from the above table.

Forest area is reported to have increased by more than 6 percent in last six years. Such a change may be attributed to three factors – firstly, in the light of Supreme Court order felling of tree in notified area must have at least been controlled to check further degeneration of the forests. Secondly, a Forestation programme of the government with plantation of exotic varieties like teak appears to have played a significant role in the extension of forest cover. And thirdly, it may be adoption of a definition that classifies many unusable lands as forest. In addition, local administration's attempt to check Jhum Cultivation, earlier through the introduction of New Land Use Policy (NLUP, 2000) reinforced through Mizoram Intodelhna Project (MIP, 2002-03), appears to have paid dividends in

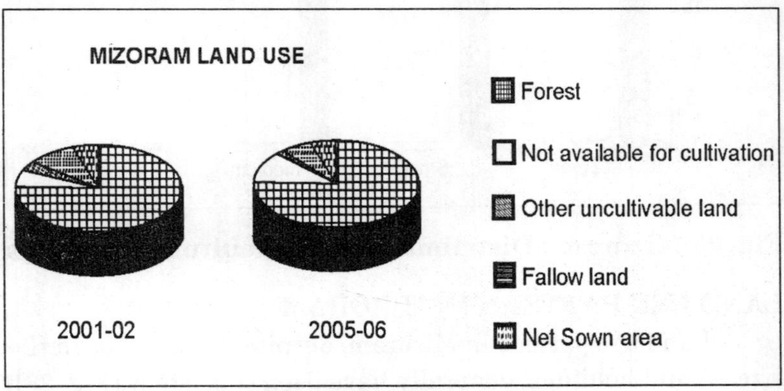

Fig. 26(a) Mizoram Land Use

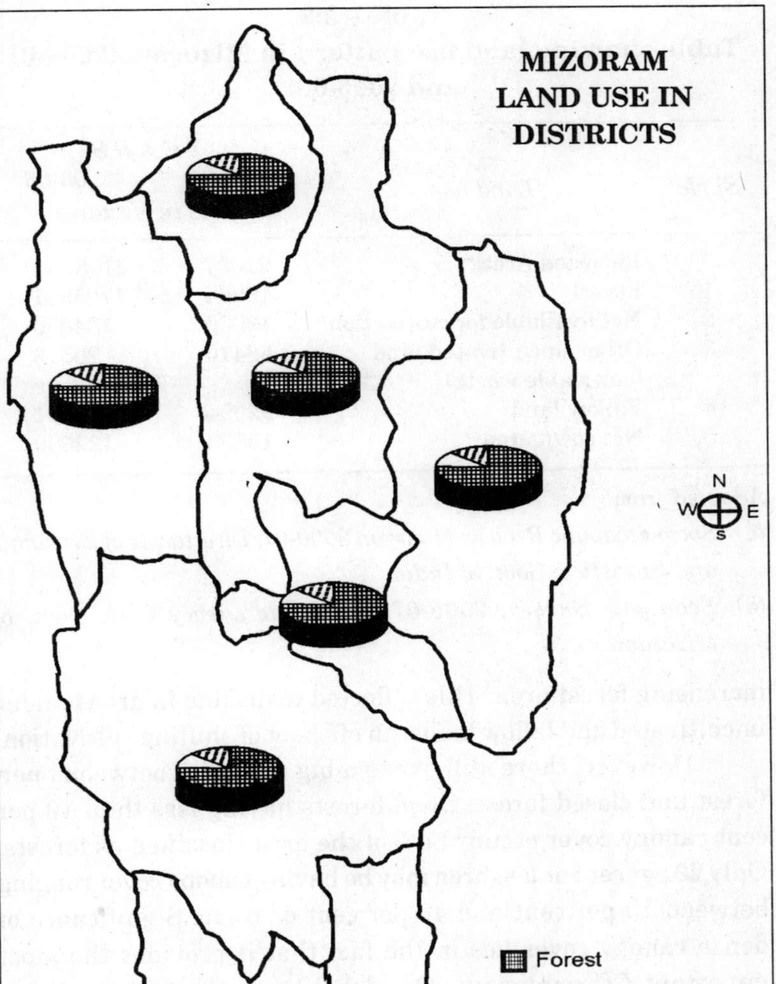
MIZORAM
LAND USE IN
DISTRICTS
N
W
E
S
Forest
Agriculture
Others

Fig. 26 (b)

Table – 3:2
Table showing land use pattern in Mizoram (2000-01 and 2005-06)

Sl.No	*Land use*	*YEARS* 2000-01	2005-06
		Area in Hectares	
	Reported Area	21087	2108700
1	Forest	16264	1725851
2	Not available for cultivation	13039	134030
3	Other uncultivated land (cultivable waste)	58410	20578
4	Fallow land	192094	106241
5	Net sown area	10133	122000

Adopted from

(a) *Socio-economic Review: Mizoram 2000-01, Directorate of Economic and Statistics, Govt. of India.*

(b) *Economic Survey, 2006-07, Economic survey Cell, Govt. of Mizoram.*

increasing forest area. This reflected in decline in areas under uncultivated and fallow lands, an offshoot of shifting cultivation.

However, there still exists a big disparity between open forest and closed forest. Open forests having less than 10 per cent canopy cover occupy 80% of the area classified as forests. Only 20 per cent or less area may be having canopy cover ranging between 10 per cent and 40 per cent or more. Significance of dense canopy cover lies in the fact that it provides the most important CO_2 sink zone. On global level, the forests absorb 62% of the CO_2 generated. Thinning of the cover certainly reduces the efficiency, hence global warming. 25 per cent of the mountainous area of the world that certainly includes Mizoram will have to play a significant role in maintenance of such efficiency.

It is true that mans' economic interests and environmental limitations more often than not, are considered to be in conflict. The conflict, however, is not so much of sustenance as it is between 'mass production and production by the mass'. Tribes the world over have been drawing their sustenance from the forests. New techniques in the field of agro-forestry and afforestation may provide them much decent life. It is significant to note that tribal societies generally have cohesive community life that is able to curb individual's greed and monopolization of resources. With large population still depending on agriculture and forest areas Mizo society with strong social structure may still show the path to live in harmony with the forests and natural settings. Efforts, however, has to be made to distinguish between capital and labor intensive endeavors. The former has been found to encourage appropriation of resources by powerful individuals and groups that brew acute economic differentiation in the society. Latter is believed to help people, in general, to participate in productive functions according to the suitability of the area and their choice albeit at lower rate of production.

Decline in the area under the categories of other uncultivated land (64.77%) and fallow land (44.69%) over 2000-01 may also be partially attributed to addition to Net Sown Area (20.40%) and other non-agricultural uses particularly built up area (2.79%). With growing significances of horticultural activities and infrastructure development, area under these categories may be expected to increase substantially in near future.

Agricultural Land Use

Despite the fact that agriculture continues to remain the most important of state's productive activity, only about 6 per cent of the total area could be put to agricultural use in 2005-06 (Economic Survey, 2006-07; Govt. of Mizoram). It was though an improvement over 2000-01 by 1.19 per cent generally the area under agricultural use has been declining since early 1990s. The state had recorded 11.7 per cent of the total area to be under different agricultural uses in 1989-90. Decline in agricultural uses of the land is though reflected in declining share of agriculture to the state GSDP it is not reflected on the dependence of the people on agriculture. Agriculture still provides employment to over 60 per cent of the workers in the state.

Agricultural land use in Mizoram, despite attempts to control is still dominated by Jhum cultivation. As a matter of fact, area under jhum is found to be increasing (Table 3:3).

Table 3:3
Area under different types of cultivation in Mizoram

Type of cultivation	*2000-01*	*2004-05*
	(Area in Hectares)	
Jhum	52500	64536
Settled	17848	93300
Total	70348	157836

Important crops grown in jhum field include Rice, maize, pulses and oil seeds. All the crops, as is obvious, are mostly grown on subsistence basis. Little surplus that farmers may be having enters local markets and adds to their income. Total area under different crops has been reported to be around 165800 ha. in 2004-05, i.e. about 7.86 per cent of the total area where Rice cultivation dominates with 68.21 per cent as its share.

Rice is the most important crop grown in the state yet total rice production in the state meets its requirement only up to a level of 56 per cent. There does not appear to be much improvement in the situation as most of the rice is still grown in Jhum fields. As a matter of fact, the area under jhum rice increased by over 14 per cent between the year 2000 and 2005 where as jhum production of rice registered a growth of only 8.16 per cent. During the same period area under wet rice cultivation (WRC) and High Yielding Variety of rice grew by 8.11% and (-) 31.57 % with a production growth of 7.63% and (-) 38.31% respectively.

This requires a serious consideration on the part of the farmers as well as the agricultural administration. Expansion of area under jhum (particularly for rice cultivation) may though partly be attributed to increasing population, failure in increasing area under high yielding varieties or desired expansion under WRC is no less responsible.

It must be realized that success of high yielding variety of seeds is dependent on certain necessary inputs viz. sufficient and controlled supply of water and appropriate fertilizer doses. In the physical condition prevailing in Mizoram probably the two conditions are difficult to be met. If at all such conditions are met the cost incurred may be prohibitive at least for the farmers. At the same time, wet rice cultivation in the state is handicapped by shortage of irrigation facilities. It is obvious from the fact that most of the crops are cultivated as rain fed kharif crop. Hardly 4 per cent crop may be classified as rabi grown mostly during dry winter season. Growing such crops require artificial supply of water i.e. irrigation. However, only 3 per cent of the total agricultural area has the facility of irrigation. Naturally, therefore, the years having good rainfall also coincide with good harvest in the state. Lack of irrigation facilities also restricts diversification of crops and increase in their yields. As a result the area under Kharif crops particularly under food grains has been rising (see table 3:4)

Recently, however, horticulture has been gaining in significance. Orange, banana, passion fruit, areca nut, ginger,

Table: 3: 4
Comparative area under different crops in Mizoram (2000-01 and 2004-05).

Crops	*2000-01*	*2004-05*
	Area in Hactares	
Rice	51839	107661
Maize	6643	19788
Pulses	2374	7971
Oil seeds	7375	5321
Horticulture Crops	-	14777
Others	2117	10253

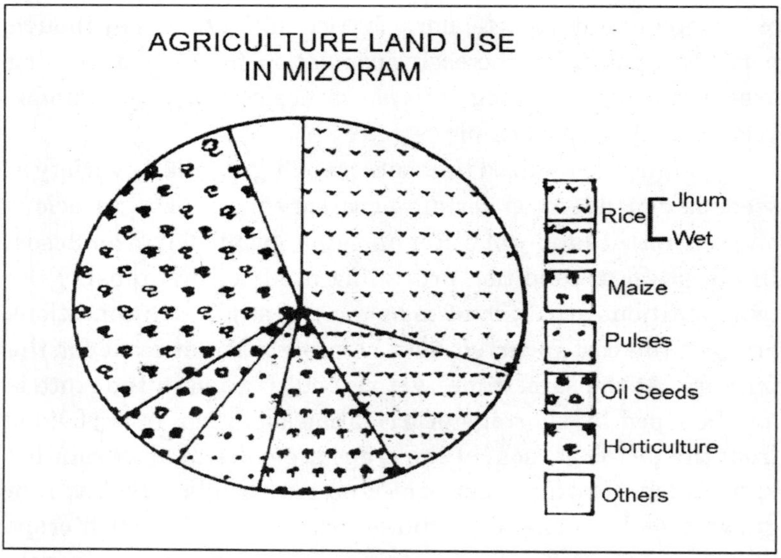

Fig. 27

chili and green turmeric are the major horticulture crops in the state. They may be viewed to provide a new dimension to state's agriculture. Suitability of the land for these crops is proved beyond doubt. What they require is a commercial thrust. It may be achieved by bringing down the cost of production, improving transportation, storage (for perishable products), and packaging facilities. Other alternative may be value addition to the products through different processing techniques. Quality control of the products will enable them to compete with products from other parts of the country.

Once commercial viability is explored and marketing assured, the farmers in the state will be encouraged and will try to shift from 'low return' traditional cereal growing practices to more gainful horticultural activities. This may also expand job opportunities for unskilled and semi skilled workers in the rural areas if large commercial production is obtained. The examples may be had from apple orchards of Himachal Pradesh, grape, orange and banana production in Maharashtra, Mango, lichi and banana production in Bihar and many like them.

Commercialization of horticultural products may also contribute substantially to state exchaquer.

Agricultural Landuse at Substate Level

Trend of agricultural land use in different districts is no much different from that at state level in Mizoram. Of course, terrain attributes and accessibility to populous urban centers and the markets appear to have influenced intensity of colonization of suitable land for agricultural uses marginally in some districts. Fig. 28 reflects the general land use pattern in Mizoram at district level in 2005-2006.

It may be noted that four districts of Kolasib, Serchhip, Lawngtlai and Saiha are conspicuous with regards to general land use albeit for different reasons. The four districts have lesser area under forest cover than the state average. In case of Kolasib and Serchhip, it may partly be explained by relatively larger colonization of land for agricultural purposes and expansion of built up area. The same may not be true for the districts of Saiha and Lawngtlai pre dominantly rural districts with lone urban center of Saiha. The two districts have less than 70 per cent area under forest cover with only 4.61 and 2.86 per cent respectively under agricultural uses. And though 3 to 5 per cent area may fall in built up category, almost 25 per cent of their territories do not appear to have been put to any productive use. Topography of the area and smaller population may be responsible for non-use of the land resources at least partly. But with diminishing area under permanent pasture (consequent upon lesser significance of livestock particularly cattle rearing with local tribes) and fallow land (due to attempts on controlling jhum practices) there does not appear any attempt to put the land under optimum use. This may partly be attributed to limitations faced by local farmers to expand agricultural colonization. The condition prevails despite the fact that the state adopted Integrated Wasteland Development Projects (IWDP) and Watershed Development Projects in Shifting Cultivation Areas (WDPSCA) with allocations over Rs. 4.40 lakh and 2000 lakh respectively during 10th plan period from the

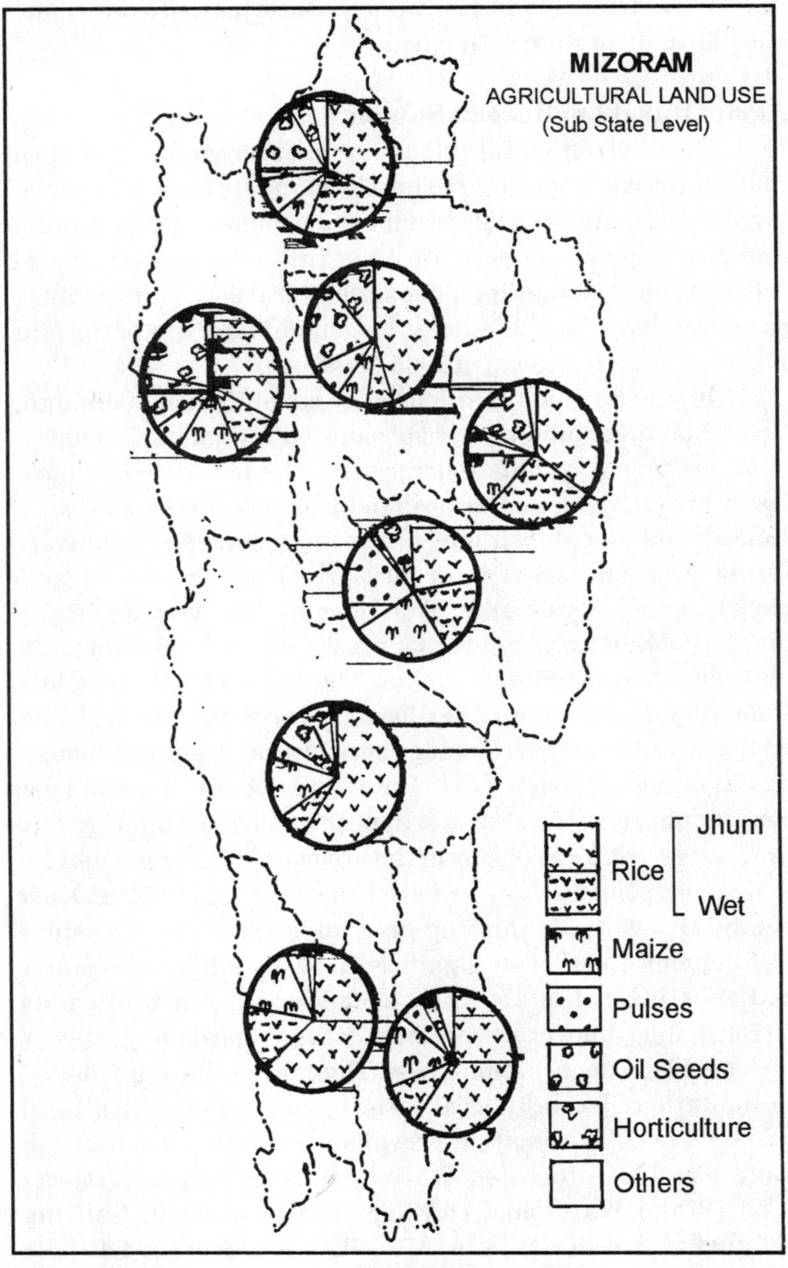
MIZORAM
AGRICULTURAL LAND USE
(Sub State Level)
Rice
Jhum
Wet
Maize
Pulses
Oil Seeds
Horticulture
Others

Fig. 28

Central Government and 40 lakh for IWDP from the State Government. Besides National Watershed Development Projects in Rain fed Areas (NWDPRA) adopted in Mizoram since 1990-91 attracted a fund allocation of Rs. 3600 lakh during the same period. The two districts accordingly were expected to develop over 23200 hectares and 18600 hectares land respectively during the same period. The results, however, do not appear to be in accordance with the expectations. In northern and centrally located districts of Kolasib and Serchhip, it appears that the project might be having certain positive impact.

Agricultural practices at sub-state level similarly show very little variation. Over 70 per cent of agricultural land in the state is still given to traditional crops (Fig. 27). Success of horticultural crops in recent times, however, indicates an attempt by the farmers to diversify, more notably in three northern districts of Aizawl, Champhai and Mamit. They together account for more than 76 per cent of the state's total area under horticultural crops and farmers appear to be adopting the practice as a subsidiary to cereal crop farming. This may largely be attributed to relative ease of access to big urban centers of the states as well as to interstate market through Cachar Plains of Assam. Further diversification in the form of adoption of sericulture, pisciculture with a nominal area of 33.2 hectares and 2580 hectares respectively and floriculture despite potentials has yet to find acceptability amongst the farmers.

The fact, however, remains that despite inducement to change; traditional subsistence farming dominates in all the districts of Mizoram. Rice cultivation remains the most dominant activity. It is aided by the fact that jhum cultivation with its monoculture characteristics is mostly given to rice cultivation. Area under Wet Cultivation (WRC) despite proclaimed attempts; remain dismally low with the exception of three districts of Kolasib, Champhai and Serchhip. Even in these districts WRC accounts for less than half of the total area under rice. This is also obvious from the fact that only 0.13 per cent of the gross agricultural area so far enjoys the facility of irrigation despite elaborate institutional and financial arrangement. One means or the other may irrigate, as a matter of fact, about 58638 hectares of land identified below 10 per cent slope. But only 26.76 per cent of the aforementioned could be brought under irrigation. It leaves much to be desired. More so when one knows that people in some parts of the state particularly in Champhai valley have had facilities of irrigation even before India attained its freedom.

It is evident from the above figure that rice cultivation continues to dominate agricultural scene in Mizoram. It is also apparent from the figure that, the districts of Lunglei, Saiha and Lawngtlai have much higher proportion of land under rice cultivation than their northern counterparts. Yet hardly 56 per cent of state's requirement, by government accounts, is met by local production. That too when rice yield per unit area in Mizoram is reported to be significantly higher at 18.86 quintal per hectares against national average of 17.33 quintals per hectares.

Maize is the second most important crop raised in the state. It is believed to off set rice shortage partly. But this is also raised only as a subsistence crop. Thus, very little quantity enters even the local market. This may also be noted that like rice proportion of area under maize cultivation is again higher towards southern Mizoram. Mamit and Champhai also have considerable area under Maize. However, maize, which may be grown two times in a year in other parts of the country, mostly has single harvest in Mizoram.

Area under pulses is generally very less in all the districts of Mizoram with the exception of Serchhip where over 1/5th of the cultivated area is given to pulse cultivation. Lesser thrust on pulse cultivation may, to some extent, be attributed to the food habits of the people and lesser demand at local level. Oilseed cultivation, on the other hand, appears to have found better acceptability in areas with undulating topography. Thus, Kolasib, Mamit and Lunglei proportionally have much more area under oil seeds than other districts.

Adoption of horticulture, particularly growing fruits and vegetables is a function of their marketability and capacity to compete with interregional products in terms of quantity, quality and cost of production. Development of horticulture in Mizoram is relatively a new phenomenon. The practice appears to have found some kind of acceptability amongst the local cultivators. Its present success, however, may largely be attributed to large subsidies and financial assistance that government generally offers to distract them from much maligned jhum cultivation. How far it can be sustained will ultimately depend on their compatibility, acceptance and sustained supply to regional and national markets either in their raw form or semi-processed/processed form to add value to the products. In fact, by their very nature most of the popular horticultural products are perishable. Therefore, success of the practice will depend on how efficiently and quickly the products are reached to the market from the length and breadth of hostile terrain that dominates in Mizoram. It is obvious from the fact that it has been more readily adopted in districts with larger concentration of urban population and/or in areas with better accessibility to them and other states. As a result, the three districts of Mamit, Aizawl and Champhai together account for more than 76 per cent of area under horticultural crops. Aizawl, the state capital, is probably the largest market for local fruits whereas ginger and some vegetable especially squash enter interstate trade. Notably all these three districts have better access to the Cachar Plains, gateway to other northeastern Indian states and rest of the country.

Industry

Growth of secondary sector led by industries is viewed as a positive indicator of economic well being of a region. It helps in expansion of productive activities. It is also believed to help in enhancing productivity of man as well as the land. With ever increasing population and changing life style industries are perceived to have been providing additional means of sustenance and economic viability to different regions of the world. Process of industrialization and associated innovative technologies has also been found to have provided impetus increasingly for diversification as well as improvement in productive efficiency thereby helping economic growth of nations/regions.

Success of industrialization, however, largely depends on rational, efficient and optimal use of resources of the region where the process has to operate. And as people and their cultural attributes are the most important components of any regional resource complex, process of industrialization hence economic development must integrate them in its fold (Sen; 1995:1-24). Each developing region must, therefore, adopt strategies to industrialize in accordance with its own dispositions at least in initial phases of development (Streeton et al; 1981). However, industrialization in developing regions of the world is generally misconstrued with Post Industrial Revolution industrialization that differs from the earlier process with regard to mode and quantum of production as well as localization of industries. Pre Industrial Revolution industries thrived on the use of widely spread animate energy. And, though per unit quantum of industrial output would appear to be small diffused location of transformation and manufacturing activities carried out mostly as handloom and cottage industry, would contribute no less substantially to the overall state economy. If there existed any deficiency in quantity, it would be compensated by quality production that competition, regional specializations and pride would induce. This, prior to Industrial Revolution in Europe, made India the leading manufacturing power after China enabling the country to have 22.6 per cent share of the world GDP (Maddison,1998). And though there persisted class differences, interpersonal/inter regional disparities in income distribution were at much lower level (Das, 2002:57). The scenario started changing in Post Industrial Revolution period. Europe with change in mode of production from 'production by mass' to 'mass production', from labor intensive production system to capital intensive technological system. Such industrialization, driven and made possible by extensive-use of new sources of energy particularly fossil fuels, which, by their nature, are localized in distribution, tends to be concentrated. Thus, Post Industrial Revolution industries have been tending to have location of Weberian type. It has been leading to restructuring of space economy as 'modern industrial production' thrives on 'the existence of numerous groups or combinations of activities' (Isard and Schooler; 1956:21-22) that must be located in a manner to facilitate mass production, optimum capacity utilization and marketing. Helped by the strategy of territorial colonization of mid-eighteen century to meet the raw material requirements of emerging Western industries, the traditional industrial base of colonized territories could not hold its competitive edge. It may be observed from the fact that India had 25 per cent of global trade in textiles at the start of Industrial Revolution in Europe (Bairoch and Levy-Leboyer; 1981) and in order to off set competitive advantages of Indian textile despite the high cost of intercontinental trade, British textile industry had to seek 'protective tariffs' against it (Raychaudhury; 1983: 3-50) for its survival. In prevailing economic situation share of Indian Industrial products led by textiles came down to 1/100 of that of Britain just within a span of 150 years i.e. between 1750-1900 AD (Paul Kennedy quoted in Singh; 2003: 280).

Influenced, however, by the perceived affluence and rapid economic growth brought in by the Industrial Revolution in the West, newly liberated colonies have been attempting to emulate the model at the cost of their own conventional space economy. Scarcity of indigenous capital and modern technological skills however, made them to allow share in the use of their own resources in return of investments. Investors, on the other hand, in order to maximize their returns have been trying to monopolize the resources. The tendency may be perceived at all levels of regional hierarchy. "Powerful national states and multinational corporations" attempt to "monopolize the resources at international level, at the national level regional governments, monopoly houses and their feudal subordinates do the job" (Misra, 1982: 145-46).

The process reinforced by sectoral investments in scarce resources though generally is found to have augmented economic growth at macro level, it appears to have failed to bring about equitable distribution of income and social justice on inter personal/interregional level (Mutlu, 1991: 547-86). As a matter of fact, in Post Industrial Revolution world the disparity is found to have been growing not only in the developing regions but also in developed countries. Growing unemployment, reassertion of regional identity and resurgence of ethnicity plaguing most part of the world are examples of failure of Industrial Revolution to induce equitable economic growth hence, harmony. Thus, attempts are on to change the structure of space economy even in developed countries like the U.S.A (Cox and Mair, 1988:307-25) where some places are facing deindustrialization (Bluestone and Harrison, 1982); some experience rapid economic development (Soja et al. 1983:195-230) and some face fluctuations in their fortunes (Feagin, 1985:1204-30). Disillusioned with the existing models of economic development the restructuring of industries in the U.S has been shifting to "planning of local economic development as a means to assure some role for each locality in future space economy. Economic development, thus, is assuming a peculiarly territorialized form against the concepts of large scale capital-intensive integrated operations and corresponding views on economies of scale. Competition is induced among the localities and attributes of local capitalist firms, politicians and resultant social relations of the people are taken into cognizance. And though there may grow a competition amongst different localities, a solidarity is expected to develop amongst the members of the community of which the capitalist firms and local government institutions due to their dependence on local resources, are integral part. This has been found to enable the growth of local business coalitions that promote local economic development (Cox and Mair, 1988:307-08). It is confirmed by Mutlu (1991:547-85) after Hirschman (1958:189-95) and Myrdal (1957:31-8) that regional inequalities diminish only if and when through the market and/or by governmental design the beneficial impulses from the manufacturing sector are transmitted to ever widening circle by decentralizing industry and by modernizing agriculture under the impact of the input requirements and market needs of manufacturing.

Mizoram after attaining its statehood in 1987 has been aware of limitations of its economic base. Therefore, it undertook the problem of broad-basing its economy. It was realized that dependence on an under productive agricultural system could not meet the aspirations of its people to attain better living condition that long years of struggle for autonomy had aroused. It could not go on expanding service sector without having corresponding productive base; that neither present economic composition of workers nor GSDP reflects (see the Economy). It has, therefore, been necessary to seek additional/ alternative economic system to augment the income of the state as well as of its people. It was felt necessary to shift dependence from primary sector led by agriculture to secondary sector by enthusing people to adopt industrial activities. It was in this vein that the Govt. of Mizoram notified its first Industrial Policy on 15th March 1989 after the Industrial Policy Resolutions of the Government of India adopted during 1948-56 and their subsequent amendments in 1973, 1977 and 1983.

Industrial Policy of Mizoram, 1989 envisaged to develop its traditional industries of handloom and handicrafts, other village and cottage industries as well as some agriculture and forest resource based industries to provide its more than 52% workforce additional employment besides under productive practice of jhum farming. The policy basically aimed at all round development in the interest of the indigenous people of Mizoram by providing them with opportunities of gainful alternative employment as well as opportunities for self-employment in the industrial and allied sectors. The government also intended to bring the people of the state abreast with technology based but cost effective industries like that of electronics. However, failure of the industrial planners to plan marketability of industrial products in the world of ever increasing competition did not probably encourage local entrepreneurs to undertake ventures in which they did not have expertise. Fear of unknown could not bring the desired effect on industrial growth of the state. Barring establishment of few medium scale industries under state corporations no much industrial growth could be experienced despite positive initial responses and government's willingness to extend promotional supports in the form of subsidies and grants to private entrepreneurs. It is obvious from the fact that employment in manufacturing sector dominated by small and cottage industries grew to 2.80 per cent in 1991 from a dismal 0.85 percent in 1981, a percentile growth of over 200 percent. The high percentile growth however, appears to have been generated generally by handsome package that Mizoram received in the wake of its statehood in 1987 to rehabilitate the members of the underground outfit of yester years. It is obvious from the fact that despite continuing facilities the 2001 census recorded only 1.22 per cent of the total workforce in the state as industrial. It is obvious that availability of only home market for limited industrial output as envisaged in the first Industrial policy for the state in 1989 could not encourage the people to take up industrial production as their main vocation at any substantial scale mainly because potential for income generation in the sector was considered to be very low. Mizoram, thus, remained industrially backward and/or no industry state.

It may be this realization that prompted the government of the land to adopt a new Industrial Policy for the state in the year 2000 following the announcement of the New Industrial Policy by the Government of India for industrially backward North-Eastern Region in 1997. The policy aims at expanding industrial activities based on interlinkage of local resources mostly from agro-forestry sector. It also aims at attracting entrepreneurs and capital from outside the state as well as to "develop entrepreneurial and managerial skills by providing suitable training programme" at different levels of administrative units. Despite well meaning objectives in the New Industrial Policy of Mizoram, 2000 almost all of them apparently are capital intensive wherein strengthening of organizational set up, development of managerial skills, identification of sick industrial units and their revival and encouragement of investment from outside the state either in joint sector or private sector or both are believed to expand the industrial base. The policy statement to realize aims and objectives laid in New Industrial Policy of Mizoram, 2000 appear to be dwelling upon exogenous capital and funding as the following approaches are suggested:

1. Identification of thrust area and protection of specific industries with emphasis on (a) small and local resource based industries; (b) electronic and information technology; (c) bamboo and timber based industries; (d) development of food and fruit processing industries; (e) modernization of handlooms and handicrafts (f) industries based on plantain fiber and hill broom; (g) extraction of oil from Tung seeds and other non-edible oil; (h) family oriented tea plantation; (i) promotion of industries based on local mines and minerals (j) patronizing Khadi and village industries.
2. Fiscal and other incentive package to entrepreneurs;
3. Development of infrastructure;
4. Special promotional package for rural and traditional industries;
5. Restructuring of state public undertaking to make them commercially viable;
6. Identification and rehabilitation of sick industries meriting revival;
7. Continued improvement of training infrastructure;
8. Research and development facilities;
9. Encouraging foreign direct investment with safeguard to socio-cultural economic interest of the indigenous people.

Little seems to have been realized that most of the funds made available for such projects and their success more often than not is measured in terms of quantum of amount received as donations, aid or assistance. However they are found to be being invested disproportionately on travels, professional fees expansion of bureaucracy and 'eye catching physical structures' without having much impact on the output and broadening of the economic base (Yunus, 2007:14-17). Yunus (2007:17) further believes that dependence of states/nations on such exogenous assistance benefits only the wealthy ones directly or indirectly because the government agencies, corporations of small number of entrepreneurs as well as financial institutions favor large scale and concentrated operations for exigencies of governance and management. The functioning of the administrative machineries, thus, goes against the small operators who require small financial support but are large in number and diffused in area. It also allows powerful large firms to manipulate and appropriate resources. It goes against the participatory desire of the people and their empowerment.

Environmental considerations apart such a mindset is believed to have widened interpersonal/interregional disparities. Number of registered small scale units in Mizoram and employment provided therein corroborates the fact that despite substantial investment by the government agencies the total number of industrial units stood at 1742 in 2005-06 providing employment to only 1912 persons (Statistical Handbook, Mizoram; 2006: Table 9.1 and 9.2). Almost 1550 industrial units out of the 1742 operated without any hired worker. It is obvious from the fact that with substantial investments (a total expenditure of Rs. 1272.77 lakh during 9th plan and Rs. 7772.03 lakh during 10th plan), growth of industrial activity as well as employment opportunities in the state has been insignificant. The industrial sector has been contributing less than 1 percent to GDP and does not appear to have made much contribution to the structural transformation of the economy in the state.

TABLE : 3:5

Number of Registered Units and Proportion of Workers in Industries

District	No. of Workers	No. of Registered Units	No. of Persons employed	Proportion of workers employed in industries
Mamit	35165	44	58	0.16
Kolasib	35510	62	179	0.50
Aizawl	162961	714	1151	0.70
Champhai	68134	66	37	0.05
Serchhip	32523	85	170	0.52
Lunglei	71792	395	196	0.27
Lawngtlai	3409	125	53	0.16
Saiha	26981	248	68	0.25

Whatever may be the contribution of small-scale industries their distribution also appears to be skewed. Largest number of such industries is found in highly urbanized Aizawl district followed by Lunglei district. The two districts account for more than 63 percent of all industrial units. The following table shows district wise distribution of registered small-scale industries in 2005-06 with the number of persons employed therein and their proportion to the total available workforce in the district of Mizoram.

The table vindicates the belief that the attempt to shift the working population from agricultural activities to industrial activities is open to manipulation by powerful individuals/ groups as is obvious from the number of registered industrial units in the district of Champhai, Lunglei, Lawngtlai and Saiha. In other for districts also it appears that proportion of industrial workers does not match the total investment incurred on expansion and maintenance of these units.

The above table also clearly exhibits that location of industries and participation of workforce in them has clear urban bias. Thus Aizawl district with 73.75 percent of its people living in its four urban centers has highest number of SSI units as well as highest population of workers engaged in industrial activities (0.70%) followed by Serchhip and Kolasib having urban population over 48 percent respectively with 0.48% and 0.52% industrial workers in the same order. Number of industrial Unit may be high in the district of Lunglei at 395 but with urban population (42-23%) at relatively low-level workers' participation in industries is below 0.27%. Even in entirely rural district of Lawngtlai though the number of registered industrial units is recorded to be 125, workforce participation in them at 0.16% suggests that people find it difficult to shift to alternative activity that does not promise to improve and sustain their income.

Besides government agencies, establishment of Mizoram Khadi and Village Industry Board (MKVIB) in march 1986 under the Khadi and Village Industries (KVI) Act 1982, may also be seen as an attempt to lure people in the rural areas away from over burdened and under productive agricultural sector to industrial activities. As a result about 6825 KVI registered units were established by 2005-06 with reported employment to about 33400 persons. This alone would translate to about 9.22 per cent of the main workers against 1.22 percent actual employment under all the industries. It is, thus, obvious that employment under KVI is either overstated or at best it provides if at all only part time vocation to the people. In addition, the small scale industries including those under MKVIB appear to be engaged only in production of articles for common use at local levels. It may not require production at capacity level of the units denying commensurate relationship between investment and return. Industrial policy of the state, therefore, must not delve only upon investment it must also take into account the productivity of the industrials units, marketability of the products, employment opportunities provided by the industry and allied activities as well as inter and intra-industry linkages by encouraging split location to integrated production systems. In other word, the process of industrialization in backward regions should start with labor intensive industry moving gradually toward high tech-capital intensive activities in which the capitalists, bureaucracy, businessmen and the local communities should participate as equal partners to enhance state's capability of equitable regional distribution of the capacity for income generation.

New Industrial Policy of Mizoram has taken into cognizance the limitations that hill terrain and its fragile and susceptible ecosystem pose to development efforts. It therefore, requires strategies at implementation level. It has been a common experience that the motives of profit maximization on the part of investors, comfortable management on the part of decision makers/ managers; and urban bias of development have been source of many existing contradictions and their resultant socio-political and environmental hazards (Schumacher, 1973, 1979; Kothari, 1988). Mizoram which has been exposed to development processes relatively recently and contemplates embarking upon the path of rapid economic growth through industrialization is already abreast with the problem of disproportionate concentration of people in its urban centers influencing the social cultural make of the people and threatening the ecological stability in Mizoram.

Recent studies on global level have been showing that growth of urbanization, a concomitant of industrialization in developed world and associated activities have put enormous stress on the functioning and quality of environment. Fifty percent global population classified as urban occupy less than 3 percent of the terrestrial surface of the earth. But they are found to be responsible for 78 per cent of carbon emission, 60 per cent of total residential water use and 76 per cent of total wood for industrial and building purposes. And the impact is experienced not only at regional and sub-regional level but also at global level, due to alteration caused in Bio-geo-chemical (BGC) Cycles, hydro systems and biodiversity (Down to Earth, March 15, 2008:58). In case of Mizoram where urban concentration of population corresponds with that of the world (Kumar, 2007:6) the environmental impact cannot be any different. At the same times the space economy of the state has become uneven (Kumar, 2007) to the great dismay of the people who feel not to have been integrated in the process of development. Thus they fail to 'share a common normative behavior'.

Spread of agro-forestry resources in the state acknowledged in New Industrial Policy 2000 as the basis of industrialization in the state, therefore, requires identification of index resources and their distribution, selection of focal settlements for collection of such resources for value addition/ reducing their volume and/or weight (semi processing) to enable them to bear the high transport cost in the hill terrain. Semi-processed articles accordingly may be fully processed for commercial purposes at two or three convenient locations spread in different parts of the state. Industrialization strategy in the state must also take into its fold attainment of social justice, maintenance of ecological balance and participation of people in decision-making and implementation, for they are integral to their survival and future prospects. Misch (1977:242) and Schumacher (1979) believe that it is possible to have more people centric order upon already existing foundation. Mizoram, with a high literacy percentage, strong social institutions, large workforce and better gender parity may set pace for other developing regions of the country who also seek to attain rate of better economic growth by bringing changes in their space economy.

Infrastructure

Search for higher rate of economic growth and attempts to improve productive efficiency appear to underline the need for development of infrastructure. As instrument to improve the capacity of production systems at regional, national and international levels infrastructure development has become central to different economies of the world. Emergence of boundaryless international market in present phase of free trade and globalization has further accentuated the significance of infrastructure in making a region economically viable and vibrant. Presently the level of development (as generally propagated and understood) is considered to be positively correlated to the level of infrastructure development i.e. a system of factors facilitating expansion and choice of activities. Thus, a system of power generation, transport and communication, education and health care facilities, financial institutions, ancillary industries and governance are suggested to be fundamental to attain development objectives and enable people to improve their lot.

The driving forces behind the increasingly growing thrust for development of infrastructural facilities, however, needs to be treated with caution. No doubt, economic growth is essential to support increasing population and to meet its diverse demands. And so is its diffusion. Infrastructure development is basically believed to help the two processes. At the same time, it must be acknowledged that creation and development of infrastructure under contemporary models of economic growth, are 'capital intensive' and benefits of which may be realized only with the passage of time. There are also qualms about 'cost effectiveness' particularly when such facilities can only be maintained at exuberant costs (they appear to have an economics of their own) not only in terms of money but also in terms of environment – both human and natural.

Gregg (1958) in his comparative study established the superiority of diffused and 'labor intensive' textile manufacturing employing 'handlooms' (food-men-charkha combination) in India over capital intensive power driven localized modern industry that have led to polarization of infrastructural facilities. Factory production (supposedly more efficient than handlooms), he believes, is equipped to 'produce far in excess of the people's ability to consume'. The system, thus, is prone to wastage of resources. Productions, after all, are meant for consumption. In fact, to maintain its competitive edge such system of bulk production is unable to cut down on its productive capacity. On the contrary, it enlarges its capacity and attempts to appropriate and monopolize resources as a strategy to maintain / maximize its profitability. In the process it tends to cut down the size of its labor force hence purchasing power of the people. It leads to wastage of labor and so to inequality. Almost identical view was expressed by the great industrialist and economic thinker Henry Ford in his development discourse way back in 1926. He had then observed that "the facilities to produce are present, but these facilities are greater than the ability to consume, and there can be no peace (may be translated as development) on this earth until the ability to consume is brought up to and kept up to an equality with ability to produce. This equality can not be brought about until what is called wage motive replaces the profit motive" (Ford, 1926:152). He, even then, was advocating diffusion of economic activities and split location (for industries) to achieve this goal.

Profit motive derives its strength from selective investment(s), exploitation and unequal distribution of disposable income. It thrives on protection and subsidies as national / regional governments consider themselves vulnerable against the pressure exerted by powerful economic groups. Thus, subsidies on land, power, transportation and storage are provided. And even though they fail to address the real problem of equitable access of people to the benefits of economic growth, they may still enjoy 'tax holidays' and unlimited use of resources at the cost of tax payers' money leading to accumulation of wealth in few hands. The process appears to have aggravated in the present era of economic liberalization. It can be seen in ever increasing phenomena of unemployment and disparities in purchasing power of the people. The phenomena are observable not only in India but even amongst the strongest of the world economies. It is also found to be going against the basic tenets of democracy – social justice, freedom of choice and self respect that present world order keeps on promising. Instead, the growth of infrastructural facilities appears to be bringing about economic colonization and promoting dependency. Mahatma Gandhi had apprehended this. And so he gave the concept of 'Gram Swaraj' (Village self Governance) through self reliant economy to avoid exploitation of widely distributed rural resources by more organized and polarized urban economy. The concept also implied creation and maintenance of basic infrastructure by village communities who must generate finance for it to keep their economy going and improve the output. This, it was believed, would ensure development of facilities according to the needs and participation of people i.e. in decision making and implementation – the philosophy behind decentralization of power.

Infrastructure development besides adding to the price of commodities (by way of cost on transport, insurance, storage etc.) has also promoted diversion of resources against people who require them most. The present trend of price rise and concomitant food crisis are partly attributed to diversion of food resources like maize to production of bio-fuel to off set the growing demand for automobile fuel (Down to Earth, May, 1-15:9-10).

Development of infrastructure also facilitates and demands exploitation of hitherto uneconomical reserves of resources spread in environmentally most fragile terrains. Besides high investments in power, transport and construction sector they seem to be irreparably damaging the ecosystem far and wide (Emel and Bridge, 1995). They are found to disturb the symbiotic relationship that man as its component must have with the natural environment.

Besides, development of basic facilities in existing economic system has been a dependent variable not always to logical perception of the planners and investors. It also generally tends to impose uniformity in plan of actions. It, more often than not, is found to go against the nature of regional attributes. The problem is further compounded when the projects envisaged to be completed with certain amount of investment within a particular time frame, are not reached to their conclusive ends. It has been found to lead to escalation in revised estimates of costs which must be acceded to in order to avoid damages that an incomplete or ill designed project may cause. Unfortunately the bureaucratic as well as the legal systems that have evolved seem to favor such urges in complete defiance of the objectives they are envisaged for at the cost of tax payers' money. An example may be cited of the preparation for Common Wealth Games at Delhi that stipulated an expenditure of Rs. 1,890 Crores at the start of the mega project in 2002. Due to delays in completion of different projects under it the cost has been estimated to have over shot Rs. 45,000 Crores in May, 2010 without any signs of completion. An additional few thousand Crores may have to be invested before facilities are opened for inauguratiion of CWG, 2010 in September). With the reigning philosophy of profit maximization, very often such attempts are deliberate on the part of the policy makers, investors and managers. As a result many of the components of infrastructure development are unable to meet their obligations to help people in attaining development objectives.

Mizoram with a very distinct physical and cultural attributes, therefore, requires treading the path of infrastructure development very cautiously. Dominated by the hills of recent origin that are dotted with numerous faults and fault lines, the state falls in a medium intensity seismic zone. The hills are characterized by steep slopes comprising generally of unconsolidated rock materials. And though the state enjoys a salubrious climate a prolonged rainy season from April to October adds to the cost of creation and maintenance of infrastructural facilities. With a weak economic structure (see the economy) there is a need to link infrastructure development with internal growth of economy and generation of financial resources. More so in the present era of economic reform and globalization which have enforced review (under the pressure from world organizations like W.T.O., GATT etc.) of subsidies, grants-in aid and budgetary supports from national governments. Such financial supports are now viewed to promote parasitical economy.

The state, it is recorded, has done well in the development of its social sector but mostly with financial assistance from the central government. With a small and homogenous population, a very high literacy rate, generally good medical care facilities spread over almost all of its more than 700 villages, a very high work participation ratio of both the sexes, the state requires to review its economic policy as well as policy on infrastructure development which have been largely dependent on central devolution of resources. Such an arrangement may be considered to have created economic classes in traditionally a classless tribal society. It also appears to have encouraged concentration of population at administratively powerful centers and corresponding behavioral change reflected in consumption pattern and disintegrating conventional relationship.

Energy

In an era of 'mass production and production for the masses as the bases of new business strategies' (Kalam and Rajan, 2002:140) modern sources of energy are considered to be the fundamental resource. It also forms the basic 'infrastructure of the modern economy'. It is found to be guiding the direction of progress that development strategy of a space economy adopts. Quantum and pattern of energy use are suggested to be influencing the rate of progress and wellbeing of people in a regional complex. Ford (1926:167) was very candid when he called the present times power age, and identified its ability if rightly used with wage motive behind it to increase and cheapen production to allow mankind to have more of this world's goods. He also believed that "the way to liberty, the way to equality of opportunity, the way from empty phrase of actualities lied through power (energy). Use of modern technologies that is believed to 'propel a modern economy on fast developmental track' also largely depends on 'availability of adequate and reliable as well as affordable energy' (Singh, 2003 :155). In fact, technologies may be viewed only as a means to enhance efficiency in and diversify the application of energy (Ford, 1926:167). Thus, modern concept of development is based on productive capacity and efficient use of energy. However, its use demands caution (Kalam and Rajan, 2002:255) for, most common sources of inanimate energy by their nature are localized and limited in their distribution. They are, thus, costly in use especially in far flung areas. The modern production system that derives its strength from the use of such energy sources is generally found to be short in efficient use (particularly due to relocation of production units in developing and under developed regions consequent upon exhaustion of intensive deposits of power resources in developed world and rising cost) both monetarily and environmentally, in the exploitation of dissipated peripheral resources (Emel and Bridge, 1995:322). As a matter of fact, substituting animate sources seem to have resulted in wastage of energy. Otherwise also, many studies have shown that the use of animate source of energy compares better than that provided by fund (inanimate) resources (Gregg, 1958:3-16, 35-69) particularly in the light of psychology behind changing productive and consumer behaviors.

Besides, dependence of contemporary economic system on supply of power from such energy sources has given rise to a pattern of consumer behavior that may affect productions hence productive efficiency adversely if it (energy supply) is interrupted or is inadequate or is not affordable. This may impinge on the industrial and agricultural productions therefore, the direction of development. Similarly, use of most of the electrical appliances and electronic gadgets largely depends on the above mentioned variables. They have direct bearing on electrical and electronic industry, one of the fastest growing economic sectors influencing not only present rate of economic growth but also consumer behaviour of the people. 'Interrupted, inadequate and costly domestic supply of power adversely affects demands, therefore, production in this sector of economy (Singh, 2003:155). Realization of the significance of power in common men's life has made energy one of the highly subsidized commodity in India. But the present crisis in supply of hydro-carbon sources of energy that has engulfed the world more acutely since last decade of the twentieth century has put a telling pressure on Indian economy. In order to maintain the tempo of development there is a need to be cautious in the use and production of energy, be it industrial, agricultural or domestic (Kalam and Rajan, 2002:255).

Mizoram is generally short in power resource endowments. Yet the state is emerging as a fast growing consumer of energy resources. The dominance of road transport and galloping number of automobiles (see table: 3:6) as means of mobility for people and goods, has been leading to increasingly growing demands for petrol and diesel. The demand for kerosene oil, considered to be poor men's fuel still remains substantially high despite very large number of cooking gas (LPG) connections in the state. The following table gives trend of fuel consumption for selected items in Mizoram since 1996.

Table: 3:6
Trend of Fuel Consumption in Mizoram

Year	*Petrol*	*Diesel*	*K. Oil*	*No. of LPG Connections*
1996-97	8794	14436	4145	-
2001-02	12883	24795	7935	153061
2006-07	17553	40389	7539	180835

Source: Directorate of Food and Civil Supply, Govt. of Mizoram

Petrol consumption in last 10 years has registered a growth of about 200 percent in the state whereas diesel and K.Oil consumptions increased to the tune of 280 percent and 180 percent respectively. LPG connections in the state grew by 118 percent just in 5 years between 2001-02 and 2006-07. Such a pattern of fuel consumption in an economically under developed state assumes greater significance particularly in view of pressure on state exchequer.

Similarly, electrification and electricity consumption have also registered a significant growth in the state. Over 89 percent of the villages in the state have already been electrified. Per capita consumption of electricity at 151 KWH in 2005-06, though lower than the national average of 347 KWH/per capita, is much higher than the states like Bihar, Madhya Pradesh and Orissa which have a very large thermal energy generation potential and are major contributors to national energy grid. They also have not only potential but substantially developed hydel power generation capacity. Yet they rank lowest with respect to per capita consumption of electricity at 9.3, 51.9 and 76 7 KWH. Mizoram, thus, appears to have much favorable electricity availability despite the lack of fund resources (coal, petroleum etc.) and under development of hydel power generation capacity. Till recently, diesel had been the major source of internal generation of electricity within the state.

The state though is endowed with significant potential for the development of hydel power; ephemeral nature of most

Table: 3:7

Generation and consumption of electricity in Mizoram

Year	*Installed Capacity By types (in MW)*				*Generation Capacity By type (in MW)*				*No. of villages electrified*	*Per capita consumption*
	Hydel	*Thermal*	*Diesel*	*Total*	*Hydel*	*Thermal*	*Diesel*	*Total*		
1996-97	5.27	-	25.36	330.63	4.01	-	14.16	18.17	663	
2001-02	8.20	-	26.15	34.35	6.58	-	5.87	12.45	691	91.14
2006-07*	13.75	22.92	9.92	46.59	8.66	2.43	0.37	11.46	718	151.44

Source: Statistical Hand Book, Directorate of Economics and Statistics, Govt. of Mizoram
* Economic Survey 2006-07, Govt of Mizoram

Table: 3:8
Iimport of Electricity since 1996

Year	*Import (In MW)*
1996-07	125.48
2001-02	258.75
2006-07	389.26

Source: Ibid.

of its streams coupled with terrain conditions has been a limiting factor. As a result most of its requirement is met through the import of electricity from

It is obvious from the above table that actual generation of electricity in the state is not even 1/4th of the installed capacity. Therefore, there is much dependence on import of electricity from the neighboring states to meet the increasing requirements. It is evident from the table showing the trend of electricity import in the state between 1996 and 2006.

Demand for electricity in Mizoram, however, is dominated by domestic consumption followed by Public Water Works and Commercial establishments. Almost 68 percent of the electricity available to the state is consumed by the households spread in its 89 percent electrified settlements. Electricity in the houses is exclusively used for lighting and increasing use of electrical equipments. A study by the students of Geography Department of Mizoram University in 14 villages of 5 R.D. Blocks of Aizawl district in 2006 revealed that over 62% of the villagers owned electrically operated radio and audio systems, 39% of them had television sets and more than 25% were making use of refrigerators. It is a reflection of changing consumer behavior based on electric supply in rural Mizoram.

Commercial establishments and public lightings with almost 7% and more than 5% respectively but mostly in towns are other significant consumer of electricity. But use of electricity as a means of production and enlargement of industrial base is almost non-existent. It is reported that only a little over 1.5% of electricity available finds industrial use in the state. The pattern of electricity consumption, thus, belies the national pattern of use which is dominated by the industries (over 38%) followed by domestic use and irrigational requirements of 23.52% and 23.47% respectively. Only with respect to commercial use Mizoram and national pattern compares at par.

Distribution of Electricity At Sub-state Level

Despite the fact that over 89% of the villages in Mizoram are electrified distribution pattern of the facility is highly uneven. Variability in distribution of electricity may partly be attributed to the hostile terrain where houses have to be located according to topographic dictates. This has been found to have led to widely dispersed location of houses even within the same settlement. This causes connectivity and maintenance problems that can be resolved only at a very high cost. Secondly, even though electricity is highly subsidized in India as well as in Mizoram its unevenness may also be attributed at least partly to the inability of the people to bear the cost without much of its productive use. The two aspects –accessibility and cost, are reflected in distribution pattern of electricity distribution in the state.

It may be seen that the distribution of electricity in the state is very much skewed. Intensity of electrification is found to vary from a high of over 90% in the Blocks of Aibawk (96.56%), Tlangnuam (96.21%) and Darlawn (93.56%) to a low of below 20% in Chawngte Block (18.80%). In addition, in four Blocks of Lungsen, West Phaileng, Lawngtlai and sangau less than 50% houses have power connections. As a matter of fact, 10 of the 22 R.D. Blocks have electricity connections below the state average of 75%. This, as a surrogate indicator may reflect the rate of shift to modern ways of living measured very often in terms of the use of power based durable items and per capita consumption. Electrification along with its corollaries may also be considered an indicator of quality of life and a measure of inter-regional as well as intra- regional disparities. It comes out very glaringly in case of Mizoram which on state level compares better than the national average of 86.8% rural

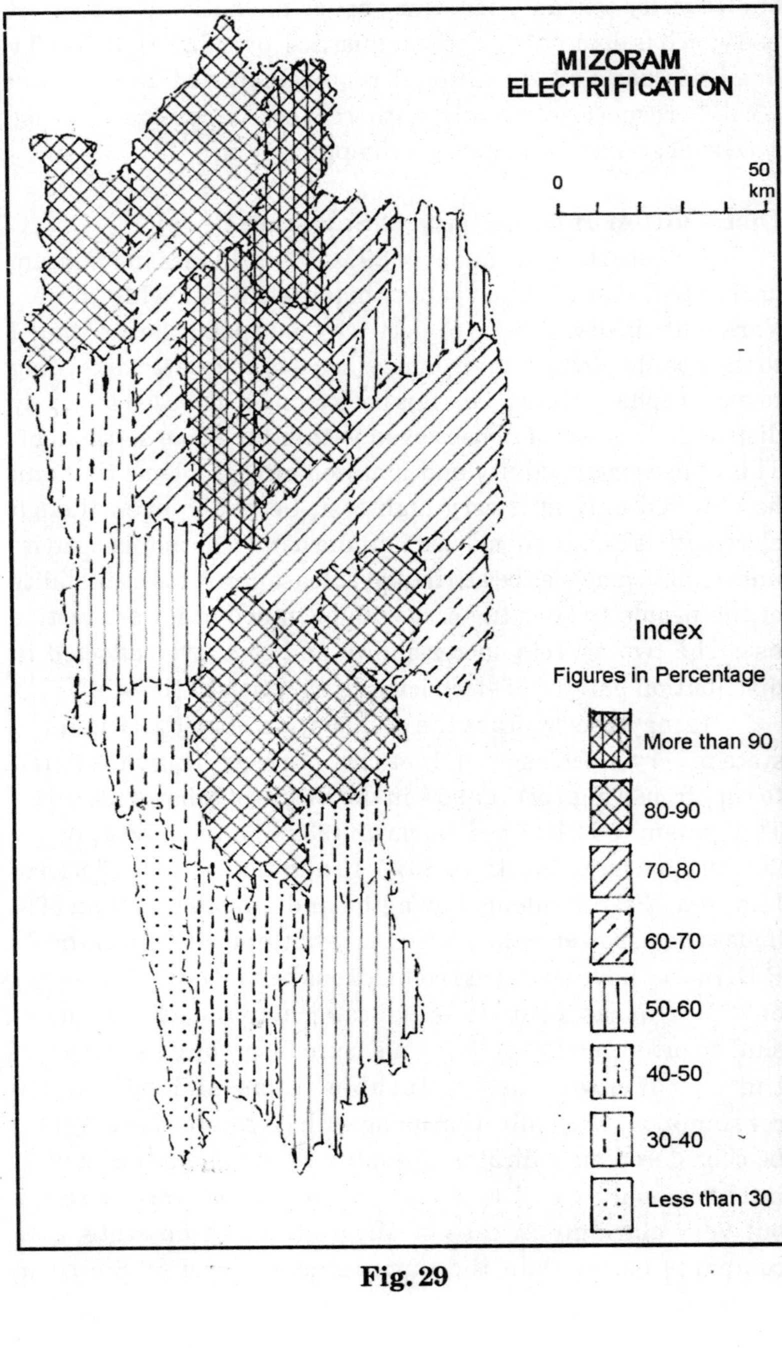
MIZORAM
ELECTRIFICATION
0
50
km
Index
Figures in Percentage
More than 90
80-90
70-80
60-70
50-60
40-50
30-40
Less than 30

Fig. 29

electrification. The spread of electricity at state level, it is a matter of concern, has, however, not been able either to boost entrepreneurship or industrialization. It is more obvious in half of the Blocks which together house almost 30% population of the state. Contribution of electricity as an infrastructural facility, thus, appears to contribute very little to economic productivity of the state in real terms.

Transport and Communication

Innovations and developments in the sphere of mobility of people, goods and information have brought about, to adopt Harvey's phrase, a 'time – space compression' (Harvey, 1990). Modern transportation systems have brought the physical space closer together. On the other hand, revolution in the field of electronic media as a means of information dissipation has carved a niche for itself. Thrift (1995) refers to it as 'electronic space'. They together appear to have induced 'hyper mobility of a new space of flow' that is leading to internationalization of economic processes and emergence of a complex interconnectedness amongst the world spatial systems. It has, therefore, become increasingly difficult to identify them as independent entities (Thrift, 1995:18). They also manifest themselves in reorganization of global space that has been undergoing rapid changes at smallest areal units (Harvey, 1989; Jameson,1991; Castells,1993). Descombes (1993) considers intensity of this interconnectedness and there growth as 'barometer of modernity' that measures the level of development. The forces though not new (they have been on unveil more prominently since middle of the 18th century, in the aftermath of the Industrial Revolution in Europe), have attained a magnitude that is giving way to 'space of flow' at unprecedented scale. It is reflected in gradual but certain detachment of dominant organization from social constraints of cultural identities and local societies (Castells, 1989:6). And, though the present trends in infrastructural development has brought about economic growth at global and national levels as never before, it appears to delve upon growth of inter- and intra-regional disparities. Added to this are huge environmental costs that the uses of new technology (facilitated by developments in means of transport and communication) are found to induce due to greater use/ misuse/ disuse of physical resources (Emel and Bridge, 1995:32). At the same time, their delicate operational systems that require constant vigil, have been found to take its toll on human health and life on one hand and enormous financial losses in case of slightest interruptions even for small periods of time on the other. Additionally, they are found also to have led to emergence of a kind of economy that warrants concentration of population defying social and cultural space. Such centers of human agglomerations though are considered melting pots they are also found to be emerging as the places of growing conflicts fuelled mostly by competition and individual/ group's search for identity (Sen, 2006). Infrastructure led accumulation of economic activities also requires 'transfer of production across world regions' that more often than not, leads to political conflicts (Taylor et.al.,1995:5-6) more visible since the second half of the previous century.

Contradictions of economic space and regional units appear to be more pronounced in developing world both at national and sub-national levels, where they are found to be proportional to accessibility in terms of physical distance and information availability.

Development of modern systems of transport and communication in Mizoram is relatively a new phenomenon. Till the middle of the 19th century people of the area had generally been secluded in the womb of the hills. The first frequent interaction of the people of this hill tract with British India probably started on a confrontational note when a group of Mizo tribal attacked a tea garden at Alexandrapur in Cachar Plains. The attack resulted in death of a British citizen and abduction of his six year old daughter, Mary Winchester in 1871. As a measure of reprisal, expeditions of British armed troops were mounted against the Mizos that ultimately culminated in occupation of the Lushai Hills in 1895.

In order to protect its own citizens as well as untoward exploitation of the hill tribes, the British administration introduced 'Inner Line Permit' under the provisions of Bengal Eastern Frontier Regulation 1873. Basic objective behind this was the maintenance of their political relationship with the tribal group and containment of militancy without disturbing the traditional political and social institutions of the Mizos. Thus, there had not been much of an effort on the part of the British administration to develop the area economically on modern lines. As it appears area connectivity had never been a priority in the scheme of the rulers of the area. Sporadic movements of administrative personals, if required, could be made by using bridle path. Most of the missionaries in their efforts to spread gospel also used the same paths.

As a matter of fact, development of transport and communication system in this part of the country was never considered seriously till 1950. There had been many reasons for underdevelopment of this basic infrastructure in the region. Initially, the area did not appear to have economic potentials that had attracted the colonial powers to other parts of the country. Categorization of the Lushai Hills as 'Excluded Area' in 1935 by the Interim Government of India did not help either simply because it did not allow such an area representation in the Provincial Legislature. Thus, provisions of expenditure for such areas in Provincial Budget could not be placed before the legislative Assembly for discussion. Later, fluidity of political situation just before Independence made the environment for such development still worse. There existed divergent views amongst the tribal leaders particularly in hill areas of north eastern India, with regard to emerging political organization of the country. Few of them were for joining The Indian Union whereas some contemplated opting for Pakistan. A third view suggesting to be part of a 'Protectorate under British crown' also prevailed. Yet there was a fourth group that strived for

'Free independent sovereign tribal state' status (Kyndiah, 1999:43).Echo of the later could be heard in the insurgent movements that engulfed this part of the country since late 1950s and persists even today in some quarters. All these factors, however, might have contributed together to place the area under low priority category for infrastructure development in general.

Significance of development of transport and communication in strategically located these parts of the country could not be realized till the Chinese aggression of NEFA (North Eastern Frontier Agency, now Arunachal Pradesh) in 1962. Gravity of the problem of under development of the means of mobility in Mizoram was further underlined when famine, in the aftermath of Mautam struck the state in mid-sixties and relief measures could not be reached timely to the people. Thousands suffered. Translating it as negligence of the state and national governments a strong contingent of the Mizo tribal took up arms and led the cessions movement under MNF leadership. Identification of areas under erstwhile East Pakistan as training centers of insurgent outfit and their south east Asian as well as Chinese connections through Burma (Myanmar) further emphasized the need and significance of developing road network (the only plausible mode of transport for bulk of mass and goods movement in the hills) to mount successful counter offensives. Volatile political situation in Burma under military rule and freedom struggle of Bangladesh and its separation from Pakistan in 1971 also reinforced the need for having a good linkage in strategically sensitive state of Mizoram bounded by international boundary on three sides. Again, in the present era of economic liberalization it has been realized that the state has the potential to provide India a profitable trade linkage to Southeast Asian countries to make it a significant player in world economy. The potential can be harnessed only through the development of connectivity within the state. In post independence period, particularly after Union Territory status in 1972 and subsequent statehood in 1987, however, there has been substantial progress in transport networking in Mizoram despite the fact that there exists little potential for rail and water ways development in the state.

The state has been brought on rail map of India since 1991 by connecting Bairabi in northern foot hills of the state with Katakal railway junction in Cachar Plains. The rail connection though might have facilitated the movement of bulky and cheap commodities to the door steps of Mizoram it is noteworthy that it runs for only 1.5 kilometers within the state boundary. Naturally, significance of railway as a means of transportation within the state is limited. With an airport near the capital city of Aizawl the state also has been having air connectivity to rest of the country since early 1980s. The two modes of transport, however, facilitate movement of goods and passengers only at a limited scale. The state though has potentials to develop water ways at least in small stretches, it is generally considered difficult and unprofitable. Thus, very little attention has been paid on harnessing this mode of transportation. However, if early history of the state is any indication (use of River Karnphuli in western part of the state to mount armed expedition against Mizo tribal by the British administration and navigation of River Tlawng by early missionaries) water ways may still provide a cheaper means of mobility in many parts of the state. Proposal of opening trade route through River Chhimpuitui in southern part between Kawlchaw in Saiha district and the Sea port at Sittwe in Myanmar underlines the significance of water ways as a means of transport. Potential for the development of water ways in the state, therefore, requires to be explored. It may still provide connectivity to settlements to supplement road system in areas where construction of roads may either be difficult due to physical conditions or uneconomical.

Road Transport

Road transport due to its inherent flexibility provides wider range of mobility and reach. It, growingly, has emerged as reliable and safe delivery system for any volume of passenger and freight extending services to almost door steps of the clients. The system is capable of handling any amount of goods and passenger even 'in high gradient terrain' of the hills. Its efficiency is enhanced by its personalized nature and minimum of legal formalities. As a result, the road transportation despite higher cost has emerged as most important means of mobility at national levels. Its significance has increasingly been realized in India both at national and sub-national levels. It is estimated that 'over 70% of passenger and 60% of freight traffic is handled by róads' in our country (Singh, 2003:265).

Significance of developing road system in harnessing the economic potential of the country was realized as early as 1943 under 'Nagpur Plan'. The Plan envisaged that no village in the country should be left untouched with respect to connectivity and proposed a Twenty Year action plan. It proposed differential approach for villages in agricultural and non-agricultural regions. The villages in agricultural region (due to dominance of agriculture in national economy) were suggested to be brought within 3 km. of one kind of road or the other to connect a major/ trunk road within 8 km. from it. The distance of villages from a link road and major road in non-agricultural region was proposed' on an average' to be within 33 km. and 10 km. respectively. The Plan envisaged achieving the target by 1963. Implementation of the Plan could not be concretized due to unique political situation that prevailed in India just before its independence. Yet the 'Nagpur Plan' provided the blue print for action that national government undertook successfully after the reorganization of states in 1956. Government of India undertook another Twenty Year action plan in 1961 and set a target to have 32 km. of roads per 100 sq. km. of area and to bring each of the more than 7 lakh village in the country within 6.5 km. of one kind of road or the other by 1981. By 2002 India managed to bring the density of road to 101 km./ 00 km^2 at national level. The same, however, could not be attained in different states of the Union. There exist big discrepancies at sub-national levels.

Kerala presently has the highest density of road with 387 km./00 km^2. On the other hand, the state of Jammu and Kashmir which has been politically and militarily sensitive has only 11 km. of road per100/km^2 of area, the lowest density of road in the country at state level. Density of road, however, is a dependent variable to the number and density of settlements. Large uninhabited areas do not attract road connectivity. In addition, condition of roads and their maintenance with respect to seasonal variations in weather determine the accessibility. Kerala having all its villages connected with all weather roads again top ranks amongst the Indian states. On the other hand, Arunachal Pradesh where roads are the only mode of transportation has only 11% of its villages connected with all weather roads.

Road transport, however, assumes paramount significance in hill terrains like that of Mizoram where it provides the only economically viable mobility to passengers and commodities. The state till late 1950s suffered mostly due to sparse connectivity. Destabilizing effects of the famine of mid 1960s and following political movement brought to the fore the significance of developing suitable transport facilities in this remote part of the country. The realization led to rapid development of road system in the state. It has made impressive strides in developing different types of roads particularly since Union Territory status in 1972.

Road transport despite physical constraints has evolved as life line for the settlements located even in the remotest part of the state. Almost all of passenger and freight traffic in the state is dependent on road transport for internal movement.

From a mere 1150 km. total road length in 1971 the state presently is served by 6060 km. of different kinds of roads providing linkage to settlements of different hierarchy. Distribution of road at 29km/00 /km^2 (2007) in Mizoram is still one of the sparsest in the country and is far short not only of the national average of 101 km./00 /km^2 it has lower density even than many of the North eastern states (see table: 3:9).

Table: 3:9

Distribution of Roads in the States of NE India

States	*Road Length (in km.)*	*Density of Road*	
		km. /00km²	*km / lakh persons*
Arunachal Pradesh	18365	22	1683
Assam	89486	115	336
Manipur	11434	51	479
Meghalaya	9565	43	415
Nagaland	21021	123	1057
Sikkim	2019	29	374
Tripura	33547	335	1051
Mizoram	**5075**	**24**	**570**

Source: http:// en.wikipedia.org./Indian Road Network (2002)

Table: 3:10
Length of Different Types of Roads in Mizoram

Category of Roads	*Quality of Roads (Length in Km.)*		*Total*
	Surfaced	*Subsurfaced*	
National Highway	1669	158	1827
State Highway	52	109	161
District Roads	1471	1243	2714
Town Roads	187	104	291
Village Roads	148	808	956
Mizoram	**3527**	**2421**	**5948**

Density of road, however, is a reflection only of the pattern of distribution of settlements for; roads are constructed primarily to connect them. There may be large uninhabited tracts where linkage may be inconsequential. Due to unique arrangements of hill ranges and settlements in Mizoram, therefore, length of the roads has to be limited. It also may not be environmentally desirable. Therefore, service to specific number of people may be considered a better measure of connectivity. In this respect, it is estimated that almost 680 km. of road in the state serve one lakh people against national average of 245 km. / lakh persons. Mizoram appears to be much better placed than many large states in the country for example Bihar has only 92 km road available to serve one lakh people. In fact, none of the major states has more favorable ratio (W. Bengal with114 km.; U.P.150 km.; Delhi 207 km.; Andhra Pradesh 259 km.; Tamil Nadu 267 km.; Maharashtra 276 km.; Karnataka 289; and M.P. 319 km to serve one lakh people have very high pressure on their roads). Even in Kerala, with most dense road network, only 474km. of roads are available to serve every lakh of persons. This average in Mizoram is also higher than many of the Northeastern states (see table 3:9) despite the fact that these states have better availability of roads than most constituents of India. Also, over 80% of its 700 villages have transport linkage in the state whereas only 43.5% of villages in the country are having road connectivity. Present thrust on developing road system in the country and realization of significance of Mizoram as gateway to Southeast Asian countries with regard to international trade, are expected to improve the linkage of settlements and its quality in the state further.

Structure of Road System in Mizoram

Development of road transport due to its 'inherent flexibility' is guided by its capacity to connect wider areas that are variable in their human organization and economic potentials. Some areas/places assume greater significance in the hierarchy of settlements at national level whereas others may be important at sub-national and local levels. They, however, require having linkage to realize equitable distribution of national resources to help people of big metropolises and smallest settlements alike to facilitate easy access to commodities of their requirement. In order to enhance efficiency of the system at national, state and sub-state level, therefore, agencies at different levels of administration are involved in planning, construction and maintenance of roads. Thus, National Highways built to link all the major cities and traversing the length and breadth of the national territory, are constructed and maintained by central agencies under national government. Similarly, State Highways are under the purview of the state governments and are aimed at connecting important settlements within the state. In the same vein, district administration attempts to create road network to provide linkage to lower order settlements within their jurisdiction as well as with settlements of higher order at state level. Inter- village connectivity; on the other hand, is generally looked after by local administration viz. Zila Parishad (District Council).Thus, there exists a hierarchy of road system in India.

Construction and maintenance of roads in Mizoram is also organized accordingly. Roads constructed by different agencies function in tandem to provide people better conditions of mobility within as well as beyond the state. Many central government sponsored schemes like 'Food for Work'; JRY; IRDP; PMGSY etc. have also helped in state government's endeavor to extend road services. Table: 3:10 Shows the length of roads constructed and maintained by different agencies at state level in 2006.

Total road length, however, registered a growth of about 2% in just one year between 2006 and 2007. The road length increased from 5948 km. in 2006 to 6060 km. in 2007. This brings to the fore the significance attached to the development of roads in the state (Fig. 30).

One National Highway (NH 54) connects Mizoram with Cachar Plains of Assam till almost to its southern tip. The

Highway is mostly aligned on the Kawnpuii-Aizawl-Hmuifang Range of hills till it crosses R. Chhimtuipui in Saiha district where it terminates on the western slopes of Phangpui Range at Tuipang. Two other National Highways (NH 44 and NH 150) connects the state with Tripura in the northwest and Manipur through Churachandpur in the east. Both of the roads have been constructed transverse to the general alignment of the hills in Mizoram. These roads have been constructed and are generally maintained by Border Road Organization (BRO). NH. 54 is particularly important and is considered life line of the state. Many of the big settlements are located along this road. Importance of this road is reflected by the fact that 7 of the 22 towns including the capital city Aizawl are located along this road. Lunglei and Saiha the two other important townships in southern Mizoram are also connected to this road respectively by NH 54A and NH 54B – the two subsidiaries of NH 54. In addition there are numerous big villages along this road. These settlements along NH 54 account for almost half of the total population of the state.

State Highways providing access to most of the district headquarters and many headquarters of R. D. Blocks also link them with the National Highways. Besides, District Roads and Village Roads which mostly have been developed as All Weather Road, provide additional connectivity to different settlements. Mizoram, despite scope for improvement, thus, may be said to have made substantial progress with regard to developing its road network particularly since statehood in 1987.

Distribution of Road at Sub- State Level

There, however, exists big disparity in respect of accessibility and linkage at district and R.D. Block level in the state. The following table shows length of roads under state P.W.D., their density and availability per lakh people at district level in 2006.

It is clear from the above table that none of the districts except Aizawl has distribution of roads in relation to area at par

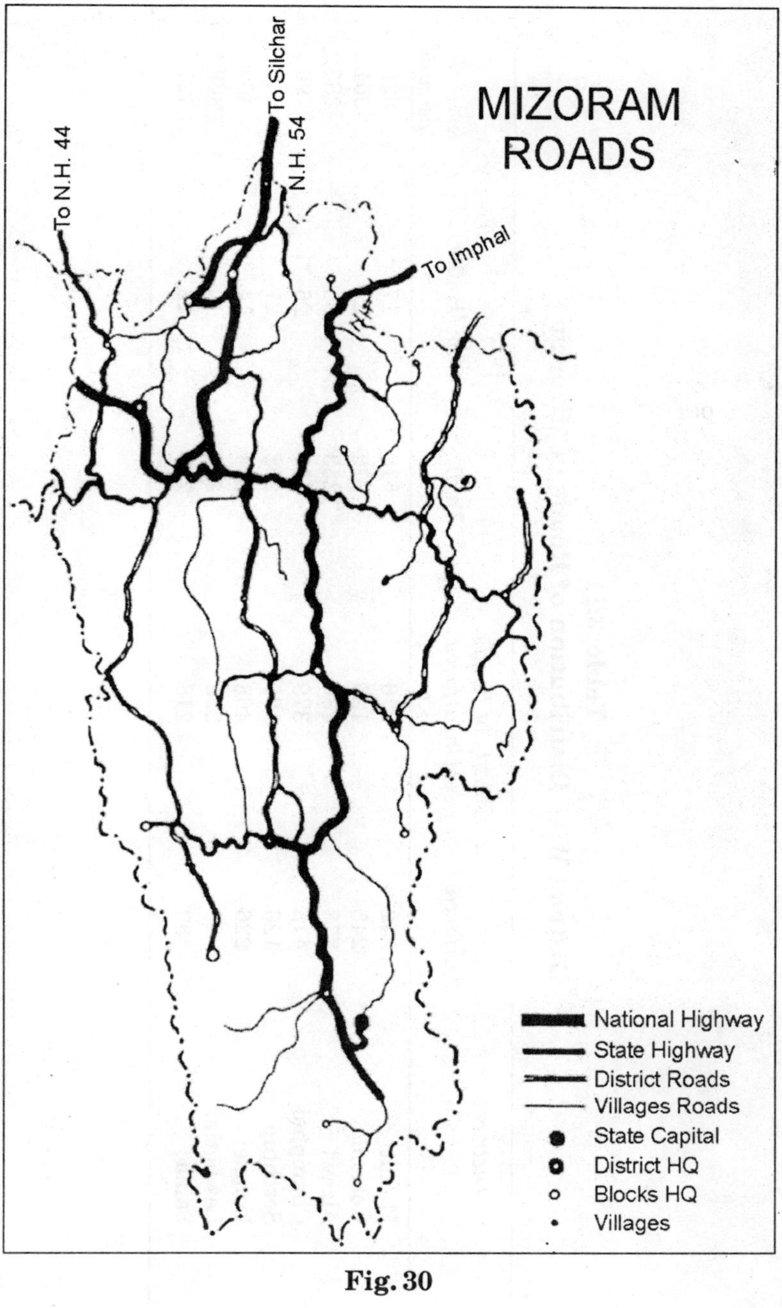
MIZORAM
ROADS
To Silchar
N.H. 54
To N.H. 44
To Imphal
National Highway
State Highway
District Roads
Villages Roads
State Capital
District HQ
Blocks HQ
Villages

Fig. 30

Table: 3:11
District Wise Distribution of Roads in Mizoram

District	*Quality of Roads*			*Density*	
	Surfaced	*Unsurfaced*	*Total*	*km / km00²*	*km / lakh persons*
Mamit	242	276	518	17	825
Kolasib	245	125	370	27	561
Aizawl	773	480	1253	33	385
Champhai	478	379	857	26	790
Serchhip	126	166	292	21	540
Lunglei	226	408	634	14	462
Lawngtlai	29	238	267	10	363
Saiha	39	218	257	18	421

with the state average. Kolasib and Champhai districts which are closer to the state average are also perceived to be proportionately developed. In fact, density of road / 00/km^2 also reflects the relative level of development at which different districts are placed at state level. Better accessibility in the state, therefore, does not seem to have encouraged diffusion of gainful activities hence lack of opportunities for people in areas of their respective abode. It, on the contrary, seems to have facilitated and accelerated internal migration to big urban centers particularly to the capital city of Aizawl which alone has to accommodate over 28% of the total population of the state. This leaves scope either for the manipulation of wide spread resources by powerful groups at state level or their under utilization. More often than not, it is found to reinforce the creation of economic classes against Mizo traditions. As a matter of fact, spread of transportation facilities must bring about dispersal of economic activities to avoid concentration of population that puts undue pressure not only on natural resources but also on available infrastructure, administrative institutions and social organization of the place. It is mostly caused by attitudinal and behavioral change induced in emerging milieu. It is also more obvious in tribal societies under transformation. They embrace new developments as a symbol of social status mostly without understanding the limitations of ecological conditions of the place/area they live in. It is noteworthy that development in the field of transportation in Mizoram has also brought about rapid increase in the number of automobiles. In fact Mizoram is recorded to have one vehicle for every nine persons above the age of six years, one of the highest ratios not only in the country but also on global level. And though on state level it does not appear to pose any threat to roadways presently, traffic problems are becoming gradually more and more acute at bigger urban centers led by Aizawl. There is little scope for expansion of roads due to terrain conditions yet vehicular movements are on unprecedented rise in towns of Mizoram.

Table: 3:12
Growth in number of motor vehicles in the state since 1971

Year	*No. of Vehicles*
1971	72
1981	817
1991	8365
2001	29224
2008	58252

As obvious from the table: 3:12 the phenomenal rise in the number of vehicles though may be an indicator of improving economic conditions of people in the state it increasingly is becoming a problem for transport managers especially in big townships. Growth in vehicular movement, in addition, is consuming path ways at the cost of large mass of pedestrians and their safety. If a study carried out in national capital (Down to Earth, May 16-31, 2008:32-35) is any indication then light motor vehicles (cars and two wheelers) that constitute 84% of motorized vehicles in Mizoram would be able to transport a meager 33% of all commuters in the state using 96% or more width of two lane roads. In a hill terrain such conditions are difficult to be met. Added to this is problem of parking not only during work hours but also during nights. Roads become parking lot in already congested towns.

Unprecedented rate of use of light motor vehicles is found to have reduced mobility leading to higher consumption of fuel and consequent fume emission and rise in air pollution, a bigger adversary of healthy mountain environment. It, therefore, is essential on the part of the users as well as transport authorities to review management of vehicular movements particularly in densely populated urban centers.

Telecommunication

Growth of modern telecommunication system in India as a means of over all development is a relatively new phenomenon.

Telephones though were in use even before India attained freedom, were considered an item of luxury and not of necessity till mid 1980s (C.M. Stephens, Communication Minister, Govt. of India in Parliament quoted in Das, 2002:208). The observation also reflects pre 1980 attitude prevailing in the country. As a result, there existed around 2.5 million telephone connections concentrated mostly in major cities, only 12000 public telephones for over 700 million people of the country adding to inefficiency and corruption in telecom administration (Das, 2002:2007). It is to the credit of Sam Petroda, an Indian American electronic Engineer and later head of the Telecom Commission of India during late Rajiv Gandhi's tenure as Prime Minister that telecommunication started being organized on modern lines. He could convince the government of the profound effects of this technology to bring about "openness, accessibility, accountability, connectivity, democracy, decentralization" that could form the basis of "effective social, economic and political development". He also could successfully propagate the view that "it was not so much wealth that created telephone density as telephone density created wealth" (quoted in Das, 2002:207). He had been instrumental in bringing paradigm shift that revolutionized the telecom industry. Presently, it is considered to be a basic infrastructural requirement. This is reflected in the fact that more than 1.25 million jobs could be created with over 5 million new public call offices by 1998. At the beginning of the present century, over 5.25 lakh villages in the country could boast of having telephonic links. With relaxation in licensing rules under economic reform policy of the government telephones, cellular mobile and internet providers have brought every nook and corner of the country within split second reach. India has also carved its niche as a major manufacturing base and exporter of telecom equipments. Yet India lags behind in providing telephone connections and generating capacity of wealth creation. The country is estimated to have a meager 2.5 numbers of telephone to serve 100 persons against a world average of 10.5 phones/00 persons.

With the spread of facilities, however, telecommunication is increasingly becoming greater in importance than transportation. The system is expected to reduce passenger transport gradually because most of the travels in connection with business, administration or social obligations may be rendered redundant. Reduction in demand for passenger movement is likely to create additional freight capacity to transport system. Despite capital intensive nature of telecom system and its fragility, it is also believed to save time, money and energy that may be used to enhance work efficiency hence productivity and accelerate development processes.

Wide spread use and need for developing telecom system on modern lines is relatively new to Mizoram. It is obvious from the fact that though telephone facilities were available in the state even before 1971 they were limited to a handful of government offices. General public had access to the facility only through three Public Call Offices (P.C.Os.) - each meant to serve about 111000 people. The number of Public Call Offices grew to 10 in 1981. It substantially reduced the burden of the P.C.Os yet each of them was expected to cater to the needs of 49000 persons. Even independent connections, private as well as governmental totaled to a meager 931 limited only to Aizawl, Lunglei, Kolasib and Lawngtlai. Progress of telecommunication facilities in the state, thus, has been apparently sluggish till early 1980s. People of the state, however, have shown a remarkable adaptability to innovations in the field of telecommunication and have been fast to make existing facilities insufficient. As a result of increasing demand, therefore, number of telephones increased to about 38000. By the turn of the last century the state could garner a healthy number of 564 P.C.Os and 500 internet connections. A 2005-06 survey has placed the number of land line connections in the state at 55200. They are also supplemented by 34000 registered cellular phones in the state. Telephone density, thus, has appreciably improved to 6.2 phones/00 persons considering only land lines. The availability index further improves to 10 phones/ 00 persons if number of cellular phones in use is also taken into account. In either case,

Table: 3:13
Distribution of Telephones in Mizoram

RD Blocks	*No. of Settlements*	*Population (Estimated 2005)*	*No. of Settlements with Telephone*	*No. of Telephones*
Aibawk	20	18333	3	311
Darlawn	29	32734	8	191
Phullen	12	14239	1	160
Thingsulthliah	24	35575	17	1377
Tlangnuam	93	268198	90	9972
Aizawl Dist.	**90**	**123955**	**12**	**2493**
Ngopa	15	19789	1	259
Khawbung	25	21400	1	189
Khawzawl	50	82766	10	2045
Champhai Dist.	**90**	**123955**	**12**	**2493**
Reiek	23	18263	7	489
W.Phaileng	24	24108	3	147
Zawlnuam	35	33292	4	1706
Mamit Dist.	**82**	**75663**	**14**	**2342**
E.Lungdar	11	15190	3	528
Serchhip	23	47993	5	2416

(Contd.)

(Contd. Teble 3:13)

RD Blocks	*No. of Settlements*	*Population (Estimated 2005)*	*No. of Settlements with Telephone*	*No. of Telephones*
Serchhip Dist.	**34**	**63183**	**8**	**2944**
Thingdawl	34	77261	10	3341
Kolasib Dist.	**34**	**77261**	**10**	**3341**
Bunghmun	35	19070	2	225
Hnahthial	22	26920	4	595
Lungsen	63	36371	4	270
Lunglei	60	71433	42	3954
Lunglei Dist.	**180**	**153794**	**52**	**5044**
Chawngte	71	37842	3	150
Lawngtlai	59	44811	11	1154
Lawngtlai Dist.	**130**	**82653**	**14**	**1304**
Sangau	19	17527	4	253
Tuipang	34	18918	10	3545
Saiha Dist.	**53**	**36445**	**14**	**3798**

Source: Statistical Hand Book, Directorate of Economics & Statistics, Govt. of Mizoram
* Economic Survey 2006-07, Govt of Mizoram

phone – population ratio is highly favorable in Mizoram when compared with national average of 2.5 phones/00 persons.

Distribution of telephones in Mizoram like most parts of the country appears to have an urban bias. The areas with the dominance of urban population are also the areas having larger number of telecom facilities. The following table shows the distribution of telephones in Mizoram at R.D. Block level in 2006-07.

It is obvious from the above table that the distribution of telephones in Mizoram like other parts of the country has an urban bias. People of the rural areas still lack this important facility of present times and are handicapped in making its productive use to improve their lot economically. The table clearly reflects that the predominantly rural blocks of Khawbung, Chawngte, Bunghmun, Lungsen, Ngopa and Phullen respectively with only 4; 4.2; 5.7; 6.3; 6.7; and 8.3 percent of their villages connected with telephones are poorly served in this regard. Logically the areas with poorer transport linkage should at least be provided better telecom facilities to enable the people to have some competitive edge vis-à-vis their urban counter parts. The distribution pattern of telecom facility in the state further vindicates the view that infrastructure development tends to be concentrated. This gives little chance of economic improvement to the people of the area that may need such facilities more. It is, therefore, necessary that telecom administration reviews its policy of extension of such services.

Space Economy and Regional Planning

There has been increasingly growing realization in developing world and the developed ones alike, of the significance of regional approach in over all development of a nation The realization stems from the acknowledgement of the unique structure and development problems of different regions at sub-national levels as well as from the growing interpersonal and interregional disparities at national and international levels that have followed the generally accepted economic models especially in Post Industrial/Commercial Revolution period of mid-eighteenth century. Such models are found to deal more with the concepts of "'utility', 'consumer sovereignty' and 'marginal products' while remaining utterly indifferent to the (social/regional) whole" (Hunt and Schwartz; 1972:7-8; Shiva; 1988:10; Rahnema; 1992:169). Such strategies though are found to have brought about small changes on micro-regional levels they could not provide resolution to disparity. In fact Schumpeter (1934 ed.: 41) had been critical of such an approach. He believed that the dynamism of economic system did not arise from consumption but from endogenous production system that could provide 'new combination of productive materials and forces. Many believe that adopted models are sycophantic expressions 'of inequality, alienation, destruction of the environment, imperialism, racism and the subjugation of women' (a statement read during the meeting of the American Economic Association, New York, Dec.1969; quoted in Hunt and Schwartz,1972:7). They thrive with political support, on 'increasing elaboration of administrative edifice, intimidating layering of organizational hierarchies and silent compliance of techno structure' demanding compliance by the people uniformly. In the process, adopting Fischer's (1964:82) expression 'the product (socio-economic and political structure) starts controlling the producer (the man) and objects become more powerful than man'. Human world is transformed into a commodity world wherein human 'labour becomes a mere tool of material production'. Maintenance of human qualities is advocated only in so far as they are meaningful to capital formation for those who control the production system. Thus, inequality, dependence and limitation of choice perpetuate. Politico-administrative systems that are believed to have evolved to safeguard the survival and economic interests of the people in different regional complexes appear not only to be crumbling but being controlled by 'parastatals, transnational corporations on international level and business houses and feudal lords at national and sub-national levels'. From being regulator of the national policies and its implementation people involved in governance at different levels, more often than not, are induced to provide interpretation of and manipulate adopted legal provisions to serve the interests of handful of powerful persons and group(s). Hegemony of interest groups working in tandem is, thus, perpetuated. Equality before the eyes of law, equality of opportunities, respect for people's choice and their dignity become rhetoric even in most respected of democracies. Dependency of larger group of common people is promoted as investment intensive strategies for development are adopted (Rahnema and Bawtree; 1997). It is found to accentuate the interpersonal/interregional disparities. 'Government of the people for the people and by the people' continues to remain a utopia in a world considered to be at highest ladder of human civilization.

Disillusioned with the existing models built upon differentials of economic growth many scholars have been seeking alternative models that may lead to more equitable and just resource utilization and income distribution hence empowerment to common man (Mahatma Gandhi was a strong advocate of such a model and 'Gram Swaraj' was its conceptualization). Regional development planning with the participation of the people in tune with the basic character of spatial resources is considered as one of the plausible models to attain the end. Regional planning as such is considered to have a prescriptive approach that imbibes in it the philosophy and strategy for mutual or 'complementary growth between different sectors of economy, areas and area levels'. The approach initially evolved after mercantilist model of economy. It was considered to be concerned only with the preparation of plan for optimal movement of the people, goods and services to effect integration of economy between producing and consuming regions. This necessitated preparation of an integrated and coordinated plan between the physical, economic and social components of a region and its different levels ranging from local to international. It, therefore, required taking into account the regional correspondence (Sundaram and Rao; 1968:109-10). Thus, Regional planning was defined as a process that attempted to integrate geographical, economic and social processes and their interrelationship in relation both to the regional space within and without. It was supposed to provide "a concrete and well organized program for sustained and integrated development of the area through active participation of and collaboration between official, non-official and voluntary agencies and the citizens" (ibid; 119).

As such the concept was adopted in India since the beginning of the 2nd Five Year Plan (the 1st Five Year Plan of India despite its commendable success in many sectors is generally believed to have been conceived as a rehabilitation plan necessitated in the aftermath of the 2nd World War and partition of the country). The Planning Commission increasingly became aware of the need for long term planning for economic development to address the problem of regional disparity in the country. Thus, a long term plan with emphasis on targets of production and investment was conceived at the start of the 3rd Five Year Plan in 1961. The long term plan (1961-76) though basically was a sectoral plan the Planning Commission felt the need to come out with clear policy statement. It stated that "the long term plan should be conceived not merely in broad national terms but should take into account the possibilities of development of resources in different regions of the country so as to spread the benefits of development as widely as possible without slowing down the growth itself" (Planning Commission; 1961:20-30). Regional considerations also found expression in the need to integrate agriculture with industry - integration of rural economy with the urban by dispersing industries and assessment of man power utilization (Sundaram and Rao; 1968:67). Unfortunately, the country is experiencing rapid urban growth without much of integration with rural economy. Not only this, the number of million cities and urban centers though has increased number of intermediate towns has been declining in India. This may be viewed as expressions of interruption in inter settlement linkage and skewed core-periphery relationship created mostly due to 'creation of new division of labor leading to national disintegration' (Sunkel; 1969, 1973). Environmental questions apart such developmental efforts in developing countries have led to increased dependence and marginality that are found to be 'driving a wedge into national society' at every level of area organization. Only a miniscule minority is integrated into such an emerging system directed mostly by transnational system of economy (Sunkel; 1972). Recent thrust on liberalization and post-development thinking for structural reform, deregulation and privatization though are propagated to enhance the rate of economic growth (traditionally equated with development) they are considered to have 'an anti-development perspective, not in terms of goals but in terms of means. The agency of development equated with economic growth switches from state to market'. Governments use their authority to 'engineer changes in favor of monetarism of the market forces 'which are deemed a failure or disaster for the majority of the population' (Pieterse; 2001:6). It vindicates the view of Sunkel.

Mizoram supposedly born out of dissatisfaction against its own marginality and dependence appears to be faced with the same dilemma revealed by different development theories. It is found to be breeding intra state marginality and dependency (see economy and settlement) in an area having by and large people of same stock and cultural background. People in different parts feel alienated as reflected in exposition of Hmar and Riang problems and demand for greater autonomy in different parts of this tiny state. Those who can afford gather near the seat of power (see urbanization). Thus there has been disproportionate concentration of population defying the dictates of environmental principles. It is also found to lead to inequity in disbursement of financial resources for which the state is dependent on unsustainable external supply (see the Economy and observation of Ray). It was this kind of fear besides security concerns that probably led the British administration to introduce Personal Residential Surcharge (PRS) at Aizawl in 1930s. Whatever might have been the cause of such legislation, it was certainly an exercise to dissuade the people to concentrate at one locale so that the remote areas are not denuded of their most important of human resource- people in working age group. Their mobility would have hampered utilization of widely distributed resources in a difficult terrain disturbing the livelihood pattern of a simpler Mizo society of those years. In post independence period, however, the situation changed rapidly. Population has been growing at a rate that indigenous economy of the state would not be able to sustain. At the same time the ruling philosophy of global economy and liberalization would not permit exogenous financial support in the form of subsidies, grants-in-aid and likes of them to continue for long (the financial instability of the strongest economies of the world in late 2008 may be indicative of the future of shape of weaker economies like that of India and its federal units). Even if such financial arrangements continue Nun (1969:201) in his study of Latin America pinpointed the problem of marginalization and surplus population ('part of which are not only afunctional but even dysfunctional' in creation of capital) as originating from the increasing control of exogenous capital and creating 'marginal mass'. Quijano (1977) identified various sources of urban and rural marginality. Creation of monopoly sector that thrives on bankrupting selected capital generating establishments; destruction of handicraft, workshop, small commerce and small service sector and introduction of capital intensive farming, he believes, lead to removal or marginalization of labour force untensifying social differentiation. Furtado (1972, 1973) believes that control of technical progress by investors of and imposition of consumption pattern from the core regions lead 'to perpetuation of underdevelopment and dependence in the periphery. The increasingly diversified consumption pattern geared towards the high- income groups in peripheral regions structures an equally diversified industrial consumer-goods production pattern' furthering the concentration of income and the surplus labor'. Such strategies though are suggested to have enhanced the rate of economic growth they have not necessarily induced development (Clower et al., 1966) as they have not been able to bring about underlying structural, institutional and qualitative changes bringing forth a positive change in country's/region's capabilities (Hogendorn,1987). Instead, lopsided growth inevitably results in 'under utilization or even non-utilization of natural and human resources to the detriment of common people who must forfeit their share of national (regional) prosperity' (Chandrasekhar, 1970:39-43).

It is in this light that Kumar (2003) proposed appraisal of composite resource (natural, human and cultural) and identification of their association at micro level - the R.D. Blocks in Mizoram for judicious planning in the interest of common people. Based on 1991 (20 R.D. Blocks) data he adopted 18 variables (8 for natural resource, 5 for human resource and 5 for cultural resource) and identified 5 R.D. Blocks to have equitable distribution of resources; 4 having equitable distribution of human and cultural resources; 1 with dominance of natural and cultural resources; 4 having predominance of natural resource; 3 having predominance of human resource and 2 having predominance of cultural resources (Fig. 31). 15 Blocks were, thus, found to have under utilization of one resource or the other. Obviously, incidence appeared to follow the trend under the accepted model of development wherein natural resource in the Blocks of Bunghmun, Lawngtlai Chawngte and Sangau awaited use but the blocks of Lungsen, Darlawn and. Thingsultliah had heavy concentration of people without basic resources to provide a descent living. Similarly, occurrence of cultural resources represented in the study by the distribution of educational, transport and health facilities in the blocks of Zawlnuam and Hnathial were found to be under utilized in absence of proportionate number of users. Likewise, West Phaileng with relatively better concentration of natural and cultural resources was found to be short in its human resource endowments. On the other hand, Khawzawl appeared to suffer on account of ill distributed facilities. Distribution of resource association as it exists in Mizoram would suggest making a conscious effort for redistribution of resources for their optimal use. It would appear that except for the region of equitably distributed resources there are problems in resource development and exploitation in the state. As the region of evenly distributed resources has all the resource factors evenly or proportionately distributed they may be developed with relative ease. But the problem lies with the areas having two resources evenly distributed or having one predominant resource. In such areas attempt will have to be made to achieve equitable distribution.

Even in such areas the region with dominant natural and cultural resources should pose least problem as they may be said to have resources on credit side. People from dominantly human resource region may easily be persuaded to adopt such areas as they may offer better opportunity for livelihood. Thus, the Blocks of West Phaileng, Bunghmun, Lawngtlai, Chawngte and Sangau may be selected to reduce the burden of relatively disproportionate concentration of people in the Blocks of Lungsen, Darlawn, Thingsultliah and to some extent also from Tlangnuam, Lunglei, Aibawk and Reiek. Khawzawl on the other hand requires creation of more cultural resource to enable its people to use their natural resources more efficiently. Such attempts, however, require change in attitude and accordant behavior not only of general public but also on the part of local government which must look beyond the petty electoral politics. In this regard it appears that if inter regional migration is encouraged, the state may benefit doubly. Firstly, demand on natural and cultural resource will be reduced in human resource region. Secondly, migrant population may introduce better and more efficient techniques of exploitation and resource use. Such migrations are also believed to breed more harmonious relations amongst different tribal groups. With the development of transport facilities and little modification in land ownership laws such migrations may be made possible. This may also stem the flow of disproportionate migration towards the state capital.

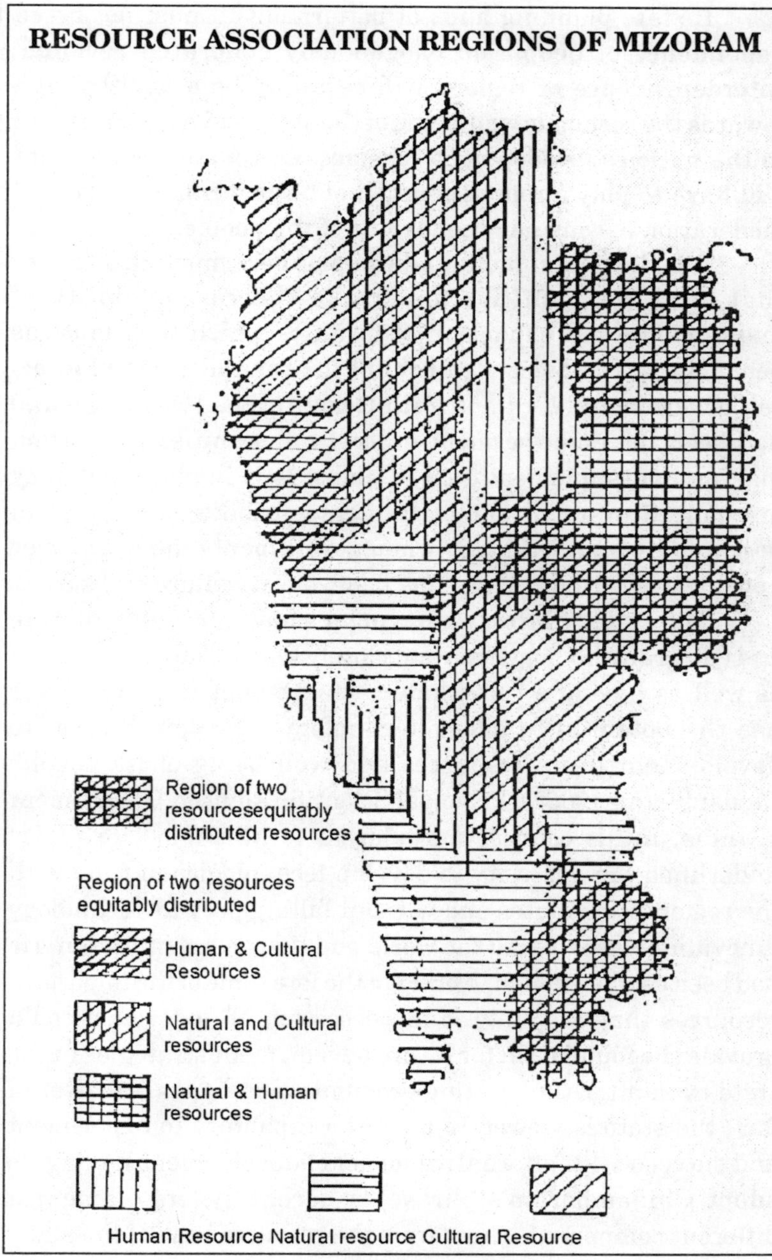
RESOURCE ASSOCIATION REGIONS OF MIZORAM
Region of two resourcesequitably distributed resources
Region of two resources equitably distributed
Human & Cultural Resources
Natural and Cultural resources
Natural & Human resources
Human Resource Natural resource Cultural Resource

Fig. 31

If state planning aims at betterment it must not breed dependence of people on exogenously generated revenue. Interdependence of regions will certainly be a healthy sign towards the economic well-being of the state and may contribute to the nation's development schemes. Of course, government will have to play a role in creation of basic infrastructure and moderation of consumer behaviour of the people.

But the government and the planners must also ensure that local communities undertake the responsibility of maintenance and expansion of facilities which they must as beneficiary. The basic idea behind the revitalization of locals self government (73rd and 74th Constitutional Amendments) had been the empowerment of local communities in decision making and implementation of plans. It is implied that they are obliged to undertake certain responsibilities. More so in post welfare state economy when governments the world over appear to be withdrawing from benevolent welfare measures.

The state of Mizoram having a small but highly literate and culturally homogenous and closely knit social organization as well as having a remarkable achievement in social sector has the potential to adopt 'technology foresight' critical to development of its resources and well being of its people. Chidambaram (2008), Principal Scientific Adviser, Government of India, in his convocation address to Mizoram University underlined the necessity to develop technologies in tune with the regional attributes and without falling prey to 'technology innovations' overtaking the world and their mere imitation. He had been candid enough to bring to the fore some of the important resources that the state is in possession of and which could provide the foundation for future development strategies in the state even after the existing economic models. As a matter of fact, the state is viewed to have the capability to experiment and succeed with alternative model of development having, to adopt Chidambaram's phrase, 'coherent synergy' amongst different components that forms the resource base of the state. It requires to be noted that different models of development have emerged only as a result of what Myrdal (1971: 4-5) calls 'recasting of economic thoughts' by 'Adam Smith, Malthus, Ricardo, List, Marx, John Stuart Mill, Jevons and Walras, Wicksell and Keynes as a response to changing political conditions and opportunities' and their followers. Development strategies suggested by these theorists delve upon sectoral investments, inequity in the use of resources, exploitation, deliberately imbalanced investments, expansion and competition (breeding interregional/ interpersonal tension, greed and jealousy) and thrive on colonization of marginal lands, manipulation of environmental resources and legal system against the basic needs and genuine aspirations of the masses. The problem appears to have arisen mostly due to capital/ investment intensive nature of suggested development models instead of labor intensive models emphasizing judicious production system. Mizoram and its people despite growing consumerism, even to day are in a position to propagate an alternative model of development in tune with Gandhi's observation that mother Earth (the Nature) is capable of meeting 'every body's need but not their greed'. People and the civil society in the state have already shown their capacity to bring about moderation in the behavior of political parties and politicians during elections to Legislative Assembly and the Indian Parliament. Electioneering in the state in which all the aspiring candidates in 2008 state Assembly elections were made to face the electorate on single platform to answer their queries directly and commit their policies. The experiment was found to have curtailed unnecessary expenditure and vulgar display of money power. Election Commission of India and other states may take some cue from Mizoram elections where people really feel to have been politically more empowered than their counter parts in other parts of the country.

It is in this light that one can extend the concept of people's participation in space economy and micro-level regional development planning. The state of Mizoram with its cultural attributes and high literacy rate has the potential to rationalize the implementation of development programs in the larger interest of the state and its inhabitants by involving people in removal of disparities of all kind for, the respect for each other, compassion for the fellow beings, idea of austerity, sacrifice and benevolence are inbuilt in the traditional Mizo value system of 'Tlawmngaihna'*.

References

Bairoch, P. and Levy Leboyer, M. (1981) : *Disparities in Economic Development since the Industrial Revolution*; MacMillan; London.

Bhat, L.S. (1968) : 'Regional Development and National Planning in India' in Proceedings of the 21st International Geography Congress; New Delhi.

Bingham, R.D. and Blair, J.P. (1984) : 'Introduction: Urban Economic Development' in R. D. Bingham and J.P. Blair (eds) Urban Economic Development; Urban Affairs Annual Review; SAGE; 27: 11-19.

Bluestone, B. and Harrison, B. (1948) : *The Deindustrialization of America : Plant Closing, Community Abandonment and Dismantling of Basic Industry*; Basic Books; New York.

Castells, M. (1989) : *The Informational City, Informational Technology, Economic Restructuring and the Regional Process;* Blackwell; Oxford.

Ibid (1993) : 'The Informational Economy and the New International Division of Labor' in M. Cornoy et al. (eds) *The New Global Economy in the Information Age*; Pennsyl. State University Press; Penn. (U.S.A.).

**The word 'Tlawmngaihna' in Mizo represents a value system that imbibes in it self respects as well as respect for others, compassion, bravery and self sacrifice without any aspiration for reward.*

Chandrasekhar, C.S. (1970): 'Balanced Regional Development : Problems and Prospects' in T.B. Lahiri (ed) *Balanced Regional Development*; Oxford and IBH Pub. Co.; Calcutta.

Chidambaram, R. (2008) : Fourth Convocation Address; Mizoram University; Aizawl.

Clower, R.; Dalton, G.; Harwitz, M.; Walters, A.A. (1966) : *Growth without Development*; Evanston; Illinois.

Cox, Kevin R. and Meir, A. (1988) : 'Locality and Community in the Politics of Local Economic Development'; AAAG; 78 (4): 307-25.

Das, G. (2002) : *India Unbound*; Penguin; New Delhi.

Dutt, R. and Sundharam, K.V. (1981) : *Indian Economy*; S. Chand & Co.; New Delhi.

Descombes, V. (1993) : *'The Barometer of Modern Reason on the Philosophy of Current Events*; OUP; Oxford.

Emel, J. Bridge, G (1995) : 'The Earth as Input: Resources' in R. J. Johnston; P.Taylor; and M.J. Watts (eds) *Geography of Global Change*; Oxford; Blackwell; pp. 318-32.

Feagin, J.R. (1985) : 'The Global Context of Metropolitan Growth; Houston and the Oil Industry'; *Am. Journ. Of Soc.*; 90: 1204-30.

Fischer, E. (1964) : *The Necessity of Art: A Marxist Approach*; Penguin; London

Ford, H. (1926) : To day and Tomorrow; Heinman; London.

Furtado, C. (1972) : 'Extrena Abhangigkeit und Okonomisch Theorie' in D. Senghass (ed) *Imperialismus and Strukturelle Gewalt: Analysen Uber Abhnginge Reproduktion*; p. 316-34; Frankfurt am Main: Surhkamp Verlag (ref. in C. Kay (1991) 'Reflection on Latin American Contribution to Development p. 47; *Development and Change*; SAGE; New Delhi; 22:31-68.

Ibid (1973) : 'The Concept of External Dependence in the Study of Underdevelopment' in C.K. Wiber (ed) *The Political Economy of Development and Underdevelopment* Random House; New York; pp. 118-23.

Ginsburg, N.S. (1968) : 'Areas, Regions and Human Organisation' in Proceedings of 21st International Geographical Congress, New Delhi, pp. 7-13.

Gregg, R.B. (1958) : *A Philosophy of Indian Economic Development*; Navjeevan Pub. House; Ahmedabad.

Harvey, D.W. (1989) : *The Condition of Post Modernity*; Blackwell; London.

Ibid (1991) : 'Between Space and Time: Reflections on the Geographical Imaginations; AAAG; 80: 418-34.

Hirschman, A. (1958) : *The Strategy of Economic Development*; Yale Univ. Press; New Haven.

Hirway, I. (1984) : 'Critique of Target Group Approach : A Study in Gujarat'; *Indian Journ. of Agri. Economics*; July- Sept.

Hagendorn, Jan S. (1987) : *Economic Development*; Harper & Row; New York.

Hunt, E.K. and (1972) Schwartz, J.G. (1972) : *A Critique of Economic Theory*; Penguin Education; Middlesex (U.K.).

Huntington, E. (1951) : *Principles of Human Geography*; John Wiley & Sons; New York.

Isard, W. (1956) : 'Industrial Complex Analysis, Agglomeration Economics and Regional Development'; *Journ. of Regional Sc.* 1:1- 22.

Jameson, F. (1991) : *Post Modernism or Cultural Logic of Late Capitalism*; Verso; London.

Kalam, A.P.J. (2002) Rajan, Y.S. : *India 2020: A Vision for New Millennium; Penguin*; New Delhi.

Kay, C. (1991) : 'Reflection on Latin American Contribution to Development'; *Development and Change* 22; SAGE, New Delhi.

Kothari, R. (1988) : *Rethinking Development*; Vikas Pub.; New Delhi.

Kumar, G. (2003) : 'Resource Association Regions : Quest for a Development Strategy– A Case Study of Mizoram' in R.N. Prasad and A.K. Agarwal (eds); *Modernization of The Mizo Society;* Mittal pub.; New Delhi.

Ibid (2007) : 'Process of Urbanization in Developing Regions: Mizoram, A Case Study'; *Geographic*; 2: 4-10.

Ibid (2007) : 'Urbanization and Changing Human *Organization of Space in Mizoram : A Case Study; Indian Geographer*; 3(5): 57-66.

Kyndiah, P.R. (1999) : *Pillars of Mizo Society*; Govt. of Mizoram; Aizawl.

Maddison, A. (1998) : *Chinese Economic Performance in the Long Run*; OECD; Paris (quoted in G. Das (2002: 56); op. cit.).

Misch, G and Patricia (1977) : *Toward A Human World Order*; Paulist Press; New York.

Misra, R.P. (1982) : 'Target Group and Regional Development' in B. Someswara Rao and V.N. Despande (eds) *Poverty*; Somaiya pub.; Bombay.

Multu, S. (1991) : 'Regional Disparities, Industry and Government Policy in Japan'; *Development and Change*; 2:547-86; SAGE; London.

Myrdal, G. (1957) : *Economic Development and Under-developed Regions*; Harper Torch Books; New York.

Ibid (1971) : *Asian Drama* (abridged version by Seth S. King) The Twentieth Century Fund; Pelican; New York.

Nun, J. (1969) : 'Superpoblacion relative, ejercito industrial de Reserve y masa marginal' *Revista*

Latinoamericana de Sociologia'; 5(2):178-235 (ref. in C. Kay; op. cit.;p. 47).

Pieterse, Jan N. (2001): *Development Theory: Deconstructions / Reconstructions*; Vistaar Pub.; Delhi.

Quizano, A. (1977) : 'Imperialismo Y 'marginalidad' en America Latina, Lima: Mosca Azul Editores' (ref.inC.kay; ibid; p. 41).

Rahnema, M. (1992) : The Post-development Reader; Zed; London.

Ray, S. (2004) : 'Fiscal Reforms and Related Issues: A Critical Assessment of Financial Sustainability in Post Statehood Mizoram'; paper presented at National Seminar on Development of North East India; Arunachal University and Instt. for Human Development; 26-28 Nov.; Itanagar.

Raychaudhury, T. (1983) : 'The Mid- Eighteenth Century Background' in D. Kumar and Meghnad Desai (eds) *The Cambridge Economic History of India*; Cambridge Univ. Press; Cambridge; Vol. 2.

Ryans, J.K. ,jr. and Shankalin, W.L. (1986) : *Guide to Marketing for Economic Development: Competing*. in America's Second Civil War; Publishing Horizon Inc.; Columbus.

Schumacher, E.F. (1973) : *Small is Beautiful; Blonds & Brigs*; London.

Ibid (1973) : *Good Work*; B. I. Pub.; New Delhi.

Schumpeter, J. (1934 ed.) : *The Theory of Economic Development*; Harvard Univ. Press; Harvard.

Schumpeter, J. (1952) : *Socialism, Capitalism and Democracy*; Thames; London.

Sen, A. (1995) : 'Rationality and Social Choice' *The American Economic Review;* 85 (1): 1-24.

Ibid (2006) : *Identity and Violence*; Penguin; London.

Shiva, V. (1988) : *Staying Alive: Women, Ecology and Development;* Zed; London.

Siddartha, K. (1999) : *Economic Geography: Theories, Processes and Patterns*; Kisalaya; New Delhi.

Singh, J. (2003) : *India: A Comprehensive Systematic Geography*; Gyanodaya; Gorakhpur.

Soja, E.W.; Morales, R. (1983) : 'Urban Restructuring: An Analysis of Social and Spatial. Change in Los Angeles'; *Economic Geography;* 52.

Streeten, P.; Burk, S.J.; Haq, M.; and Stewart, F. (1981) : *First Thing First: Meeting Basic Human Needs in Developing Countries*; OUP; London.

Sundaram, K.V. and Rao, Prakasa (1968) : 'Regional Planning in India' in Proceedings of the 21st International Geography Congress; New Delhi; pp. 109-24.

Sunkel, O. (1969) : 'National Development Policy and External Dependence'; *Journ. of Development Studies*; 6(1): 23-48.

Ibid (1972) : 'Big Business and Dependencia': A Latin American View; *Foreign Affairs*; 50(3) : 517-31.

Ibid (1973) : 'Transnational Capitalism and Disintegration in Latin America'; *Social and Ecoomic Studies*; 22(1):132-76.

Taylor, P.J.; Johnston, R.J, Watts, M.J. (1995) : 'Global Change at the end of the Twentieth Century' in R.J. Johnston; P.J. Taylor and M.J. Watts (eds) *Geography of Global Change*; Blackwell; Oxford; pp.1-10.

Thrift, N. (1995) : 'A Hyperactive World' in R.J. Johnston et al.; ibid; pp.18-35.

Vera, A. (1949) : 'Economic Development of India' (quoted in Bipin Chandra (1993) *Bharat mein Aarthik Rashtravaad ka Udvav Aur Vikas* (Hindi, 2nd ed.); Anamika; Delhi; p. 51.

Viner, J. (1958) : 'The Economics of Development' in A.N. Agarwal and S.P. Singh (eds.) *Approaches to the Problem of Underdevelopment*; OUP; New Delhi.

Yunus, M. and Jolis, A. (2007) : Bankers to the Poor; Penguin Books; New Delhi.

Index

M

N

S

T